CITYPACK GUIDE TO
Rome

Contents

KEY TO SYMBOLS

➕ Map reference to the accompanying pull-out map
✉ Address
☎ Telephone number
🕐 Opening/closing times

🍽 Restaurant or café
🚉 Nearest rail station
Ⓜ Nearest Metro (subway) station
🚌 Nearest bus route

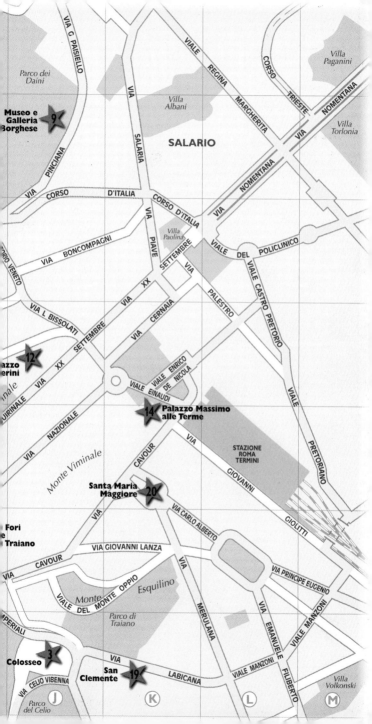

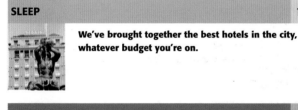

📷 Nearest riverboat or ferry stop
♿ Facilities for visitors with disabilities
ℹ Tourist information
❓ Other practical information

💷 Admission charges: Expensive (over €10), Moderate (€5–€10) and Inexpensive (under €5)
▷ Further information

Introducing Rome

Rome is one of the world's great cities, the city of the Caesars, of romance and *la dolce vita*, of long, hot, sunny days, of superb art galleries, churches and museums, of fountain-splashed piazzas and majestic monuments to its golden age of empire.

It is also a city with all the myriad pleasures of any Italian destination—notably superb food and wine—as well as great bars, cafés, and shopping, vibrant nightlife and numerous cultural events. At the same time, Rome is very much a contemporary city—traffic rumbles around medieval cobbled streets—though the skyline bristles not with glittering skyscrapers but with the domes of churches and palaces.

But how to visit a city where there is so much to see? First of all don't rush to the Colosseum, St. Peter's or the Sistine Chapel on your first morning. Rome for much of the year is hot and crowded. If you try to cram in too much, or soldier on through the heat, the chances are you'll emerge battered rather than enraptured. Instead, stroll around the Ghetto or Trastevere, two of the city's quaintest old quarters, or have a cappuccino in one of Rome's loveliest squares, Campo de' Fiori or Piazza Navona. Or head

for one of the lesser-known art-filled churches, such as San Luigi dei Francesi or Santa Maria del Popolo, crammed with masterpieces by Raphael, Pinturicchio and Caravaggio.

Once gently acclimatized, and hopefully charmed by the city's quieter side, then you can begin to think about the Trevi Fountain, the Spanish Steps, the Roman Forum or the Vatican Museums. And, of course, the newer but still relatively unsung museums that have opened in the last few years—notably the Palazzo Altemps and Palazzo Massimo alle Terme, both devoted to Classical art and sculpture, or the MAXXI gallery, an architectural *tour de force* given over to contemporary art. But bear in mind this is a living city with more than 3,000 years of history. One, two, even ten visits aren't enough to do it justice. However much you see, one thing is for certain, you'll be back.

FACTS AND FIGURES

- Population estimate in 2017: 284,700.
- The official age of Rome in 2017 is 2,771 years.
- There have been 266 popes and 73 emperors.
- The city covers an area of 1,494sq km (577sq miles).
- Vatican City covers an area of 0.44sq km (0.17sq miles) and is the world's smallest state.

SECRET KEYHOLE

Rome's most charming view is from Piazza dei Cavalieri di Malta on the Aventine Hill. To find it, go to the left of the church of Santa Sabina and to the end of the piazza; look through the keyhole of the door (No. 3) of the Priory of the Knights of Malta. Through this tiny hole you will see a secret garden and an avenue of trees framing...but let's not spoil the surprise: see for yourself.

WATERY WASTE

More than 50 of Rome's fountains are fed by the waters of the Aqua Virgo, a source that the Romans first brought into the city in 19BC. It flows from the countryside outside the city, and feeds the Barcaccia fountain at the foot of the Spanish Steps, before supplying many others, including the most famous of them all, the delightful Trevi Fountain.

SWISS GUARD

The pope's official bodyguards are recruited from Switzerland's four predominantly Catholic cantons. Each must be between 19 and 25, at least 1.75m (5ft 9in) tall and remain unmarried during their tour of duty. Their distinctive uniforms may have been designed by Michelangelo in the hues of the Medici popes—red, yellow and blue.

Focus On Bernini

Many have changed the face of Rome over the centuries—artists, emperors, tyrants and popes—but few have had a more lasting or more widespread effect on the very fabric of the city than Gian Lorenzo Bernini, a sculptor and architect whose piazzas, sculptures, follies and fountains you will encounter time and again in the Eternal City.

Papal Favor

Bernini was born in Naples in 1598, the son of Angelica Galante and Pietro Bernini, a Florentine sculptor. At the age of seven he was accompanying his father to Rome and assisting him in artistic commissions, work that eventually brought him to the attention of Pope Paul V and the Pope's affluent nephew, Cardinal Scipione Borghese. The patronage of the papacy and of wealthy Roman families such as the Borghese was the key for any artist hoping to work and succeed in Rome, especially in the era of the baroque, when the city's churches, palaces and public spaces were undergoing a dramatic transformation.

Bernini's output would be prodigious, and he would go on to work under several popes, combining undoubted talent with a shrewd awareness of how to play his wealthy patrons. In this he was in distinct contrast to his rival of the period, Francesco Borromini, a more inventive architect, but a troubled soul whose dark disposition won him few friends and fewer commissions.

St. Peter's

Bernini's mark on Rome is most apparent in its principal religious building, St. Peter's (▷ 14–15), where he designed the great piazza in front of the church, parts of the facade and much of the interior, including the colossal *baldacchino,* or canopy, above the altar. He also designed the church of Sant'Andrea al

Clockwise from top left: The Rape of Proserpina, *Museo e Galleria Borghese;* Fontana del Nettuno, *Piazza Navona;* Apollo and Daphne, *Museo e Galleria*

Quirinale and had a hand in several palaces, notably the Palazzo Barberini (▷ 36–37), Palazzo Montecitorio and Palazzo Chigi-Odaleschi. When you stop to admire a fountain in Rome, the chances are that it will be the work of Bernini, from the most prominent—the Fontana dei Quattro Fiumi in Piazza Navona (▷ 46–47)—to more idiosyncratic fancies such as the Barcaccia fountain (▷ 48–49) at the foot of the Spanish Steps, and the Fontana delle Api and Fontana del Tritone (▷ 67, 68) in Piazza Barberini.

Masterpieces

Bernini's consummate architectural skill was in creating public spaces, as in the Piazza San Pietro, or adapting existing churches and palaces in ways that were sympathetic to their surroundings. His sculptural skills—and he was the foremost sculptor of his day and the greatest since Michelangelo—were a peerless technique and the ability to capture a narrative moment in stone.

Both dramatic and dynamic qualities can be seen best in his masterpieces in the Galleria Borghese (▷ 30–31), housed in the sumptuous palace of his old patron, Cardinal Scipione Borghese. Here is David caught in the act of casting his sling at Goliath; Daphne turning into a laurel tree to escape the clutches of Apollo; and the abductor's hand sinking into the soft thigh of his victim in *The Rape of Proserpina*. These are dazzling, virtuoso works, intended to impress, but Bernini can also be witty and quiet, and it is his smaller works you'll find dotted around Rome that you may well remember best after you leave the city: the charming turtles added to the Fontana delle Tartarughe (▷ 68), for example, or his "Breezy Angels" on the Ponte Sant'Angelo and the quaint little elephant and obelisk in front of Santa Maria sopra Minerva (▷ 54–55).

Borghese; angel on Ponte Sant'Angelo; detail of the baldacchino, St. Peter's Basilica; David, Museo e Galleria Borghese; the colonnade, St. Peter's Square

Top Tips For...

These great suggestions will help you to tailor your ideal visit to Rome, no matter how you choose to spend your time.

Burning the Midnight Oil
Sit up late with the beautiful people in **Ombre Rosse** (▷ 135–136).
Share a glass of wine with the characters in the bars around **Campo de' Fiori** (▷ 44–45).
Visit one or more of the many clubs in the **Testaccio** (▷ 130, 132) nightlife district.

Saving for a Rainy Day
Buy an integrated **travel pass** (▷ 167) and save on public transport.
Visit Rome's art-crammed churches, such as **Santa Maria sopra Minerva** (▷ 54–55), they are virtually all free.
Time your visit for the last Sunday of the month (9–12.30), when the expensive **Vatican Museums** (▷ 26–27) are free.

An Evening of Entertainment
See what's playing at the **Teatro dell'Opera di Roma** (▷ 137), Rome's opera house.
Enjoy a night of blues or jazz at the long-established **Big Mama** (▷ 133).
Look out for posters advertising **church recitals** and other **classical music concerts**. In summer, many are held outdoors (▷ 130).

Romantic Suppers
Dine outdoors in summer; try **Vecchia Roma** (▷ 151), but almost any restaurant or pizzeria with tables on a terrace will do.
Splash out on a meal at **Il Convivio Troiani** (▷ 145), for that special dining experience.
Buy a picnic and take it to the **Pincio** gardens (▷ 72) to watch the sunset over St. Peter's.

Specialty Shopping
Try **Via dei Coronari** (▷ panel, 120) and nearby streets for antiques and fabrics.

Clockwise from top left: Cafés in Piazza Navona buzz at night; ruined palaces on the Palatine Hill; dining at Giggetto in the Ghetto district; enjoy a coffee at

Stroll down **Via Margutta** to take in its various art galleries (▷ panel, 120).

For designer clothes and accessories, it has to be **Via dei Condotti** (▷ 120–121).

A Breath of Fresh Air

The **Villa Borghese** (▷ 75) park offers numerous walks and shady nooks.

Escape the crowds around the Forum by climbing the **Palatine Hill** (▷ 69–70).

If you don't have time to see the Gianicolo and Villa Doria Pamphilj above Trastevere, how about the closer **Orto Botanico** (▷ 61)?

A Taste of Tradition

Giggetto (▷ 147–148) and **Piperno** (▷ 149–150) serve classic Roman-Jewish cuisine.

As its name suggests, **Checchino dal 1887** (▷ 145) has been serving traditional Roman food for more than 120 years.

To sample pizza at its best, try **Ivo** (▷ 148) and **Da Baffetto** (▷ 145–146).

A Great Cup of Coffee

La Tazza d'Oro (▷ 151), a stone's throw from the Pantheon, is a temple to the espresso.

Sant'Eustachio (▷ 150) serves what many consider to be Rome's best cup of coffee.

Antico Caffè del Brasile (▷ 142) knows its beans—Pope John Paul II once bought his coffee here.

The World's Best Classical Sculpture

Visit the **Palazzo Altemps** (▷ 34–35) and **Palazzo Massimo alle Terme** (▷ 40–41), which have beautifully presented collections.

To see individual sculptural works go to the **Musei Capitolini** (▷ 24–25), which has some of the city's most significant pieces.

The **Laocoön** (▷ 27) is the most celebrated of the Vatican Museums' immense collection of sculptures.

Sant'Eustachio; the head of Constantine in the Musei Capitolini; window-shop in style in Via dei Condotti; Bernini's elephant statue with the Pantheon behind

Timeline

753BC Traditional date of the foundation of Rome by Romulus, first of the city's seven kings.

616–578BC Tarquinius Priscus, Rome's first Etruscan king.

509BC Etruscans expelled and the Roman Republic founded.

60BC Rome ruled by a triumvirate of Pompey, Marcus Licinius Crassus and Julius Caesar.

PUNIC WARS

The First Punic War against Carthage (North Africa) started in 264BC and lasted for around 23 years. In the Second Punic War (218–201BC) Rome was threatened by Hannibal, leader of the Carthaginian army. But Rome finally defeated Carthage in the Third Punic War (149–146BC).

RELIGION

There are 280 churches within the city walls and 94 percent of Romans have had their children baptized. However, only 23 percent of Romans regularly attend Mass.

48BC Caesar declared ruler for life but assassinated by rivals in 44BC.

27BC–AD14 Rule of Octavian, Caesar's great nephew, who as Augustus becomes the first Roman emperor.

98–117 Reign of Emperor Trajan. Military campaigns extend the Empire's boundaries.

284–286 Empire divided into East and West.

306–337 The Emperor Constantine reunites the Empire, legalizing Christianity. St. Peter's and the first Christian churches are built.

410 Rome is sacked by the Goths led by Alaric I.

476 Romulus Augustulus is the last Western Roman Emperor.

800 Charlemagne awards territories to the papacy; Pope Leo III crowns him Holy Roman Emperor.

The Arch of Constantine, on the route of the marathon in the 1960 Olympic Games

Caius Julius Caesar

CAIUS JULIUS CÆSAR.

1508 Michelangelo begins the Sistine Chapel ceiling.

1527 Rome is sacked by German and Spanish troops under the Holy Roman Emperor, Charles V.

1848 Uprisings in Rome under Mazzini and Garibaldi force Pope Pius IX to flee. The new Roman Republic is defeated by the French in 1849 and the papacy restored.

1870 Rome joins a united Italy.

1929 Lateran Treaty recognizes the Vatican as a separate state.

1940 Italy enters World War II.

1960 Rome hosts the Olympic Games.

2000 Some 30 million pilgrims visit Rome for the millennial jubilee year.

2005 Pope John Paul II dies, after 26 years as pontiff, and is succeeded by Pope Benedict XVI.

2011 Technocrat Mario Monti is appointed Prime Minister to address Italy's economic problems.

2013 Argentinian Jorge Maria Bergoglio becomes Pope Francis I.

2015–2016 Pope Francis inaugurates the Extraordinary Holy Year of Mercy (Dec 2015–Nov 2016).

2016 Virginia Raggi becomes Rome's first female mayor.

WHAT'S IN A NAME

Many of Rome's street names include dates that allude to significant events in the city's history. Via XX Settembre (20 September) commemorates the day in 1870 when Italian troops liberated Rome; the city became the country's capital in the same year. Via XXIV Maggio (24 May) recalls the day in 1915 that Italy entered World War I. Via IV Novembre (4 November) alludes to the date of the Italian armistice and victory in 1918 after World War I. And Via XXV Aprile (25 April) commemorates the day in 1944 that the Allies liberated the city from Nazi rule.

Detail of the ceiling of the Sistine Chapel painted by Michelangelo

Pope Francis I was elected in 2013

★ Top 25

This section contains the must-see Top 25 sights and experiences in Rome. They are listed alphabetically, and numbered so you can locate them on the inside front cover.

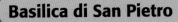

1 Basilica di San Pietro

HIGHLIGHTS

● St. Peter's Square, with its 284 columns
● Swiss Guards
● Dome
● *Pietà*, Michelangelo
● The 25.5m (83ft) 13th-century BC Egyptian obelisk, brought here in the first century AD
● *St. Peter*, Arnolfo di Cambio
● Monument to Pope Alexander VII, Bernini

TIP

● You have to join what can be very long lines for security checks (on the right side of Piazza San Pietro) before entering the basilica. Arrive before 9am.

St. Peter's combines architecture, design, decoration, art and sculpture on a monumental scale, making this vast sacred complex a fitting spiritual capital for the world's millions of Catholics.

The creators The first St. Peter's was built by Constantine around AD326, reputedly on the site where St. Peter was buried following his crucifixion in AD64. By 1452 the church was in such a state of disrepair that Pope Nicholas V resolved to build a new basilica. After several false starts it was virtually rebuilt to plans by Bramante, and then again to designs by Antonio da Sangallo, Giacomo della Porta, Michelangelo and Carlo Maderno. Michelangelo was also responsible for much of the dome, and Bernini finished the facade and the interior.

From left: The far-reaching views from the dome take in St. Peter's Square with its central obelisk, Bernini's impressive symmetrical colonnades and Rome beyond; the famous dome of St Peter's Basilica, designed by Michelangelo, is floodlit at night

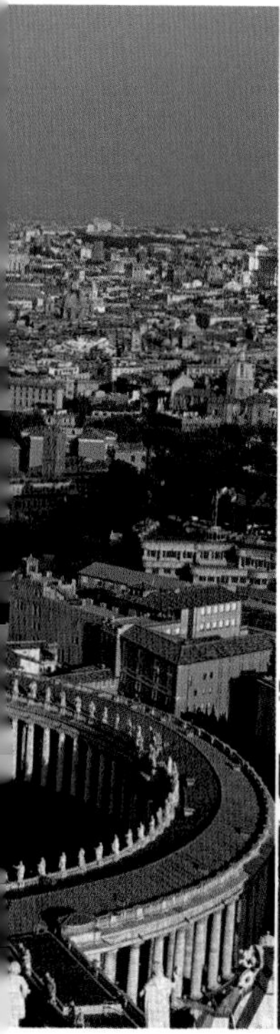

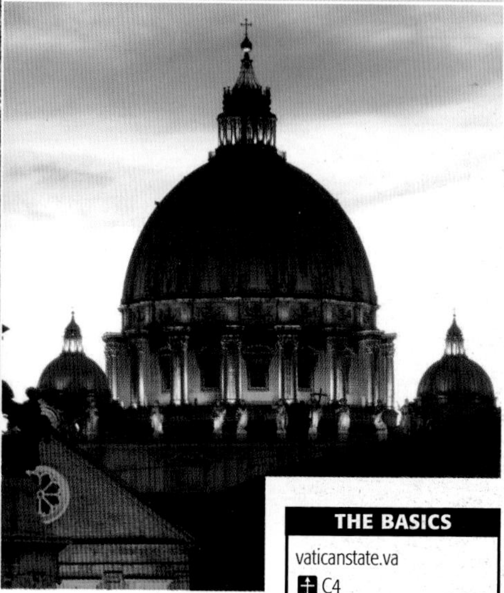

What to see Michelangelo's unforgettable *Pietà* (1499)—which is behind glass following an attack in 1972—is in the first chapel of the right aisle. On the right side of the end of the nave stands a statue of St. Peter. His right foot has been caressed by millions since 1857 when Pius IX granted a 50-day indulgence to anyone kissing it following confession. Bernini's colossal sculpted bronze *baldacchino*, or high altar canopy (1624–33), was built during the papacy of Urban VIII, a scion of the Barberini family; it is decorated with bees, the Barberini's dynastic symbol. To its rear are Guglielmo della Porta's Tomb of Paul III (left) and Bernini's influential Tomb of Urban VIII (right). Rome seen from the dome (the entrance is at the end of the right aisle, past the Holy Door) is the highlight of a visit.

THE BASICS

vaticanstate.va

C4

Piazza San Pietro, Città del Vaticano

06 6988 3229/1898

Apr–Sep daily 7–7; Oct–Mar 7–6.30. Dome: Apr–Sep daily 8–6; Oct–Mar 8–5. Grottoes: Apr–Sep daily 7–6; Oct–Mar 7–5

Shop

Ottaviano

64 to Porta Cavalleggeri or 23, 32, 49, 492, 990 to Piazza del Risorgimento

Wheelchair access

Basilica free. Dome moderate. Grottoes free

Castel Sant'Angelo, rising above the river, has served as an imperial tomb, a papal citadel, medieval prison and army barracks. Today the 58-room museum traces the castle's nearly 2,000-year history, providing a contrast to the Vatican Museums.

Many incarnations The Castel Sant'Angelo was built by Emperor Hadrian in AD130 as a mausoleum for himself, his family and his dynastic successors. It was crowned by a gilded chariot driven by a statue of Hadrian disguised as the sun god Apollo. Emperors were buried in its vaults until about AD271 when, under threat of invasion from Germanic raiders, it became a citadel and was incorporated into the city's walls. Its present name arose in AD590, after a vision by Gregory the Great, who, while leading

Clockwise from far left: The 18th-century statue atop the fortress is by Flemish sculptor Pieter Verschaffelt; the building has been a mausoleum, fortress, papal prison and museum; Ponte Sant'Angelo, the route to the castle, watched over by Bernini's angels; view of the Tiber from the terrace

a procession through Rome to pray for the end of plague, saw an angel sheathing a sword on this spot, an act thought to symbolize the end of the pestilence.

Castle and museum In 847 Leo IV converted the building into a papal fortress, and in 1277 Nicholas III linked it to the Vatican by a passage-way, the *passetto*. Used as a prison in the Renaissance, and then an army barracks after 1870, the castle became a museum in 1933. Exhibits, spread over four floors, are scattered around a confusing but fascinating array of rooms and corridors. Best of these is the beau-tiful Sala Paolina, done with stucco, fresco and trompe l'oeil. The most memorable sight is the 360-degree view from the castle's terrace, the setting for the last act of Puccini's *Tosca*.

THE BASICS

castelsantangelo.
beniculturali.it

➕ E4

✉ Lungotevere Castello 50

☎ 06 32810 (Mon–Fri 9–6, Sat 9–1) for information and ticketsonline at gebart.it

🕐 Daily 9–7.30

🍴 Café

🚇 Lepanto

🚌 30, 49, 70, 87, 130, 492, 990 to Piazza Cavour or the Lungotevere

♿ Poor

💶 Expensive; free 1st Sun of month

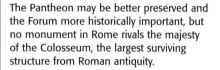

HIGHLIGHTS

● Circumference walls
● Arches: 80 lower arches for the easy admission of crowds
● Doric columns: lowest arcade
● Ionic columns: central arcade
● Corinthian columns: upper arcade
● Underground cells
● Sockets that once housed binding metal clamps
● *Vomitoria*: interior exits and entrances
● Views of ancient Rome from the upper levels

TIP

● The Colosseum's ticket office and security checks can be very busy—buy a timed entry ticket online to reduce waiting times.

The Pantheon may be better preserved and the Forum more historically important, but no monument in Rome rivals the majesty of the Colosseum, the largest surviving structure from Roman antiquity.

Awe-inspiring The Colosseum was begun by Emperor Vespasian in AD72 and inaugurated by his son, Titus, in AD80 with a gala that saw 5,000 animals slaughtered in a day (and 100 days of continuous games thereafter). Finishing touches to the 55,000-seat stadium were added by Domitian (AD81–96). Three types of columns support the arcades, and the walls are made of brick and volcanic tufa faced with marble blocks. Its long decline began in the Middle Ages, with the pillaging of stone to build churches and palaces. The desecration ended

The Colosseum takes its name from the Colossus of Nero, a bronze statue that once stood close by. The four stories above ground contained seating for spectators, while underground was a maze of corridors, cells and animal pens

in 1744, when the structure was consecrated in memory of the Christians supposedly martyred in the arena (later research suggests they weren't). Clearing of the site and excavations began late in the 19th century.

Games Armed combat at the Colosseum went on for some 500 years. Criminals, slaves and gladiators fought each other or wild animals, often to the death, and mock sea battles were waged (the arena could be flooded via underground pipes). Spectators exercised the power of life and death over defeated combatants, by waving handkerchiefs to show mercy or displaying a down-turned thumb to demand the finishing stroke. Survivors' throats were often cut anyway, and the dead were poked with a red-hot iron to make sure they had expired.

THE BASICS

archeoroma.
beniculturali.it
coopculture.it

🔒 J7

✉ Piazza del Colosseo, Via dei Fori Imperiali

☎ 06 3996 7700; online at coopculture.it

🕐 Mid-Feb to mid-Mar daily 8.30–5; mid-Mar to Mar 31 8.30–5.30; Apr–Aug 8.30–7.15, Sep 8.30–7; Oct 8.30–6.30; Nov to mid-Feb 8.30–4.30

🚇 Colosseo

🚋 Tram 3; bus 75, 81, 175, 204, 673 to Piazza del Colosseo

♿ Poor to the interior; limited access from Via Celio Vibenna entrance

💶 Expensive (joint ticket with Monte Palatino and Foro Romano)

🎫 Free 1st Sun of month

There is no lovelier surprise than that which confronts you as you emerge from the tight warren of streets around the Fontana di Trevi, the city's most famous fountain—a sight "silvery to the eye and ear," in the words of Charles Dickens.

Virgin discovery In its earliest guise the Trevi Fountain lay at the end of the Aqua Virgo, or Acqua Vergine, an aqueduct built by Agrippa in 19BC (supposedly filled with Rome's sweetest waters). The spring that fed it was reputedly discovered by a virgin, hence its name. (She is said to have shown her discovery to some Roman soldiers, a scene—along with Agrippa's approval of the aqueduct's plans—described in bas-reliefs on the fountain's second tier.) The fountain's liveliness and charm are embodied in

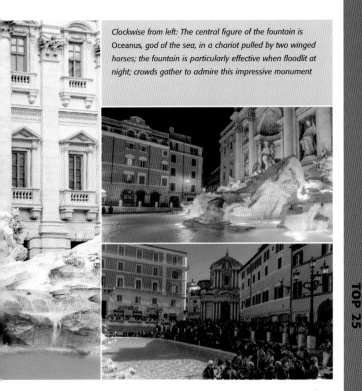

Clockwise from left: The central figure of the fountain is Oceanus, god of the sea, in a chariot pulled by two winged horses; the fountain is particularly effective when floodlit at night; crowds gather to admire this impressive monument

the pose of *Oceanus*, the central figure, and the two giant tritons and their horses (that symbolize a calm and a stormy sea) drawing his chariot. Other statues represent Abundance and Health and, above, the Four Seasons, which each carry gifts.

The fountains A new fountain was built in 1453, ordered by Pope Nicholas V, who paid for it by taxing wine. Its name came from the three roads *(tre vie)* that converged on the piazza. The present fountain was commissioned by Pope Clement XII in 1732 and finished in 1762. Its design was inspired by the Arch of Constantine and is attributed to Nicola Salvi, with possible contributions from Bernini. Those wishing to return to Rome toss a coin (over the shoulder) into the fountain.

THE BASICS

+ G5
✉ Piazza Fontana di Trevi
🕐 Daily 24 hours
🚇 Spagna or Barberini
🚌 C3, 51, 53, 62, 63, 71, 80, 83, 117 and other routes to Via del Corso and Via del Tritone
♿ Access via cobbled street
🎫 Free

⭐ 5 Foro Romano

HIGHLIGHTS

● Temple of Antoninus and Faustina (AD141)
● Colonna di Foca (AD608)
● Arch of Septimius Severus (AD203)
● Curia (Senate House, 80BC)
● Portico of the Dei Consentes (AD367)
● Temple of Saturn (AD284)
● Santa Maria Antiqua, the Forum's oldest church, dating back to the fifth century AD
● Arch of Titus

TIPS

● Making sense of the Forum is quite a challenge. Use an audio guide to get more out of your visit.
● Take something to drink, there are no refreshments sold in the Forum area. There is also little shade.

The Roman Forum was the political and civic heart of the empire—the biggest and most important forum in the world—and even now an evocative ruin. It was here, according to Shakespeare, that Mark Antony delivered his "Friends, Romans, country-men" speech after Caesar's assassination.

History The Forum (Foro Romano) started life as a marsh between the Palatine and Capitoline hills, taking its name from a word meaning "outside the walls." Later, it became a rubbish dump, then, when drained, a marketplace and religious shrine. In time it acquired all the structures of Rome's burgeoning civic, social and political life. Over the many centuries, consuls, emperors and senators embellished it with magnificent temples, courts and basilicas.

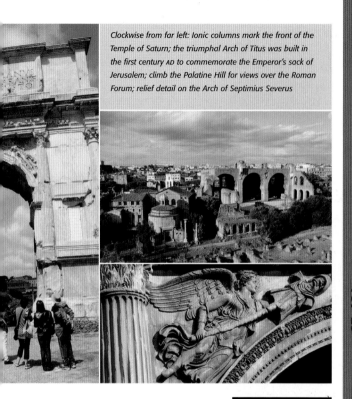

Clockwise from far left: Ionic columns mark the front of the Temple of Saturn; the triumphal Arch of Titus was built in the first century AD to commemorate the Emperor's sack of Jerusalem; climb the Palatine Hill for views over the Roman Forum; relief detail on the Arch of Septimius Severus

Forum Two millennia of plunder and decay have left a mishmash of odd pillars and jumbled stones, which nonetheless can begin to make vivid sense given a plan and some imagination. The Rostrum, the setting for Mark Antony's famous speech, provided the platform for many great historic moments.

Beauty spots Today, orange trees, oleanders and cypresses line the paths, and grasses and wildflowers flourish among the ancient remains. Somewhat aloof from the rubble stands the elegantly restored House of the Vestal Virgins (Casa delle Vestali), home of a sect formed of daughters of the Roman nobility chosen to serve Vesta, goddess of hearth and home. There were always six in number, who served 30 years from age six to 36.

THE BASICS

archeoroma.
beniculturali.it

🞧 H7

✉ Entrance at Largo Romolo e Remo on Via dei Fori Imperiali

☎ 06 3996 7700 (Mon–Fri 9–6, Sat 9–2) or book online at coopculture.it

🕓 As Colosseum (▷ 19)

🚇 Colosseo

🚌 51, 85, 87, 117, 118 to Via dei Fori Imperiali

♿ Access difficult

💶 Expensive. Joint ticket with Colosseo and Palatino

★6 Musei Capitolini

Palazzo Nuovo
● Replica equestrian piazza statue of Marcus Aurelius
● *Capitoline Venus*: life-size statue of the goddess
● The colossal statue of river god Marforio above the fountain in the courtyard

Palazzo dei Conservatori
● Caravaggio's painting of St. John the Baptist
● Bronze of *Lupa Capitolina*
● The original, restored statue of Marcus Aurelius
● Giant head and fragments of Constantine's statue

TIP
● The top-floor café, accessible without paying the museum entrance fee, offers wonderful views of the city.

The superb Greek and Roman sculptures in the Capitoline Museums (Palazzo Nuovo and Palazzo dei Conservatori) make a far more accessible introduction to the subject than the Vatican Museums.

Palazzo Nuovo The Capitoline Museums occupy two palaces on opposite sides of the Piazza del Campidoglio and are linked by an underground passage. Designed by Michelangelo, the Palazzo Nuovo (on the north side) contains most of the finest pieces. Few are more impressive than the magnificent equestrian statue of the emperor and philosopher Marcus Aurelius, which is, surprisingly, a well-made replica of the second-century AD original moved into the museum next door for restoration after damage in 1981. Among the

Clockwise from far left: The remains of Constantine's giant statue, displayed in the courtyard, include the head and a hand; the Dying Gaul, a wonderful example of Classical sculpture; visitors admire a bust of Constantine and frescoes; the Etruscan bronze of Romulus and Remus

sculptures inside are celebrated Roman copies in marble of Greek originals, including the *Dying Gaul*, *Wounded Amazon*, *Capitoline Venus* and the discus thrower *Discobolus*. In the Sala degli Imperatori is a portrait gallery of busts of Roman emperors.

Palazzo dei Conservatori As well as the Pinacoteca Capitolina art gallery and original Marcus Aurelius statue, the Conservatori is distinguished by a courtyard featuring the head and fragments of the fourth-century AD statue of Constantine, originally 12m (40ft) high. Also inside is the fifth-century BC Etruscan *Lupa Capitolina*, the she-wolf suckling Romulus and Remus (the twins were added by Antonio Pollaiuolo in 1510). Paintings include works by Caravaggio, Velázquez, Titian and Veronese.

THE BASICS

museicapitolini.org

✚ G6

✉ Piazza del Campidoglio 1 (ticket office in Palazzo dei Conservatori)

☎ 06 0608; online booking at ticket.museiin comuneroma.it

🕐 Daily 9.30–7.30

🚌 40, 44, 64 and all other services to Piazza Venezia

♿ Poor: ramped steps to Piazza del Campidoglio. Telephone in advance to 06 6710 2071 for help

💶 Expensive; combined Capitolini Card available

🎫 Free 1st Sun of month

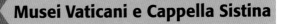

HIGHLIGHTS

● Michelangelo's fearsome depiction of God in the *Creation of Adam* in the Sistine Chapel
● *Apollo del Belvedere* (Museo Pio-Clementino)
● *Marte di Todi* (Museo Gregoriano-Etrusco)
● Maps Gallery (Galleria delle Carte Geografiche)
● Paintings in the Pinacoteca (Art Gallery)
● Room of the Animals (Museo Pio-Clementino)

TIPS

● Avoid waiting in long lines to get in by booking your tickets online at biglietteriamusei.vatican.va.
● Don't become trapped in the lines to see the Sistine Chapel—decide beforehand on your own priorities.

This is the largest, most impressive museum complex in the world, and includes one of Michelangelo's supreme masterpieces in the Sistine Chapel.

Treasures of 12 museums At least two days (and 7km/4 miles of walking) are needed to do justice to the Vatican Museums. Egyptian and Assyrian art; Etruscan artifacts; the more esoteric anthropological collections; or modern religious art—whatever your priorities, several sights should not be missed. Most obvious are the four rooms of the Stanze di Raffaello, each of which is decorated with frescoes by Raphael. Further fresco cycles by Pinturicchio and Fra Angelico adorn the Borgia Apartment and Chapel of Nicholas V, and are complemented by an almost unmatched collection of paintings

Clockwise from far left: Giuseppe Momo's spiral staircase; the Laocoön group in the Museo Pio-Clementino; Michelangelo's ceiling in the Sistine Chapel; the decorated ceiling of the Galleria della Carte Geografiche; detail of a fresco by Melozzo da Forlì in the Pinacoteca

TOP 25

in the Vatican Art Gallery. The best of the Greek and Roman sculpture is the breathtaking Laocoön group in the Cortile Ottagono of the Museo Pio-Clementino. The list of artists whose work is shown in the Collezione di Arte Religiosa Moderna is a roll call of the most famous in the last 100 years, from Pablo Picasso to Salvador Dalí and Henry Moore.

Sistine Chapel The chapel was built for Pope Sixtus IV between 1475 and 1483, but Pope Julius II commissioned Michelangelo to paint the ceiling in 1508. The frescoes, comprising more than 300 individual figures, were completed in four years. The extraordinary fresco behind the high altar, the *Last Judgment*, was begun for Pope Paul III in 1534 and completed in 1541.

THE BASICS

museivaticani.va

⊞ C4

✉ Viale Vaticano 100, Città del Vaticano

☎ 06 6988 4676

🕐 Mon–Sat 9–6 (ticket office closes at 4); last Sun of month 9–2 (ticket office closes 12.30)

🍽 Café, restaurant and shop

Ⓜ Cipro–Musei Vaticani

🚋 Tram 19; bus 23, 32, 49, 81, 492, 990 to Piazza del Risorgimento, 40 to Piazza Pia or 64 to Porta Cavalleggeri

♿ Wheelchair access

💶 Very expensive (includes entry to all Vatican museums); free last Sun of month (9–12.30)

Museo dei Fori Imperiali e Mercati di Traiano

● The view of the 13th-century Torre delle Milizie

● The intricate spiral bas-relief that climbs Trajan's Column, depicting victories in battle

● The Basilica Ulpia, which played an important role in the Imperial City, dedicated not only to religion but also to justice

Like the burgeoning Roman Empire itself, the city's uncovered remains continue to grow, even into the third millennium when this fine museum opened and more of the surrounding area was excavated.

Trajan's Markets The Mercati di Traiano were originally thought to have been the precursor of modern shopping malls—a group of commercial buildings constructed in the second century AD as a semicircular range of halls on three levels. Two of the levels survive in excellent condition. But it's now thought the "markets" were probably a new hub for politics and justice inaugurated by the Emperor Trajan in AD112 before his death in AD117, and the 150 or so booths and halls of the structure were actually administrative offices once populated by civil

Clockwise from far left: The large complex known as Trajan's Markets, where Romans gathered to conduct business; a lone column by the 13th-century Torre delle Milizie; shop fronts in Trajan's Markets; carved reliefs on Trajan's Column recall the emperor's battles

servants, though some at ground level may have been shops. Either way, they present a magnificent spectacle.

Museum The labyrinthine museum within Trajan's Markets is an absorbing peep into Rome's past. It presents the grand Imperial Fora using modern techniques, including film and pictographic illustration, as well as items unearthed in recent excavations in the area. The external viewing gallery gives a splendid view, not only of the surrounding ruins, but the whole Fora area of ancient Rome, as well as the AD113 Trajan's Column, which stands at 30m (100ft). Additionally, since 2008, the Museo dei Fori Imperiali has been a venue for contemporary arts, with regular displays of paintings and specially convened exhibitions.

THE BASICS

mercatiditraiano.it
✚ H6
✉ Via IV Novembre 94
☎ 06 0608; online tickets ticket.museiin comuneroma.it
🕐 Daily 9.30–7.30 (last admission 1 hour before closing)
🚇 Cavour
🚌 H, 40, 64, 70, 117, 170 and other routes to Via IV Novembre
♿ Good
💶 Expensive

● Antonio Canova's fine
sculpture of Paolina
Borghese (1804), who was
Napoleon's sister and the
wife of Camillo Borghese.
She is shown bare-breasted
and looks every bit as
seductive in marble as she
was in real life

The Galleria Borghese may be small, but
what it lacks in quantity it more than makes
up for in quality. The gallery combines
paintings and sculptures, including many
masterpieces by Gian Lorenzo Bernini,
Raphael, Caravaggio and others.

Bernini sculptures The Villa Borghese was
designed in 1613 as a summer retreat for
Cardinal Scipione Borghese, nephew of Pope
Paul V, who accumulated most of the collection
(acquired by the state in 1902). Scipione was
an enthusiastic patron of Bernini, whose works
dominate one floor of the gallery. His *David*
(1623–24) is said to be a self-portrait, while
Apollo and Daphne (1622–25), in the next
room, is considered his masterpiece. Other
Bernini works include the *Rape of Proserpina*

From left: Canova's reclining statue of Paolina Borghese is a highlight of the gallery; Bernini's Rape of Proserpina *depicting Proserpina, Pluto (the god of the underworld), and Cerberus the three-headed dog (the guardian of the underworld);* Boy with a Fruit Basket *by Caravaggio*

(1622) and *Truth Unveiled by Time* (1652). The statues are complemented by some of Rome's most beautifully decorated rooms.

The setting The museum is in the grounds of the Villa Borghese (▷ 75), north of the city. It is Rome's largest public park—80ha (200 acres) with five museums, gardens, lakes, fountains and a deer park. Before Cardinal Scipione made the grounds the base of his 17th-century pleasure palace, they were vineyards.

The paintings Foremost in this collection are works by Raphael *(The Deposition of Christ, 1507)*, Titian *(Sacred and Profane Love, 1512)*, Caravaggio *(Boy with a Fruit Basket* and *Madonna dei Palafrenieri, 1605)* and Correggio *(Danaë, 1530)*.

THE BASICS

galleriaborghese.it
✚ J2
✉ Piazzale del Museo Borghese 5
☎ 06 841 3979; obligatory reservations 06 32810; tosc.it
🕐 Tue–Sun 8.30–7.30; closed public holidays
🚇 Spagna or Flaminio
🚌 63, 92, 223, 360 to Via Po, or 53, 910 to Via Pinciana, or C3 to Via delle Belle Arti
♿ Steps to front entrance
💰 Very expensive

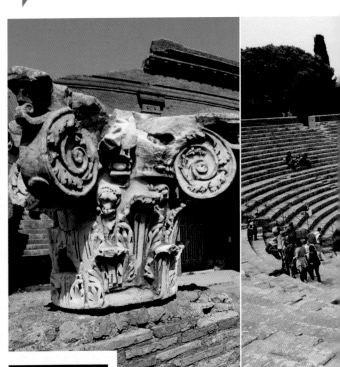

HIGHLIGHTS

● The Museum
● Piazzale della Corporazione
● The Baths of Neptune
● Casa di Diana

TIPS

● Allow a whole day for the site; perhaps bring a picnic.
● In summer, take water with you and rest in the shade during the early afternoon.
● Buy a plan of the site and spend time when you arrive planning your visit.

Imperial Rome's port is one of the three best-preserved ancient towns in Italy. More than a historical treasury, Ostia's ruins invoke an intense visual sense of the past.

Living history Less celebrated than Pompeii or Herculaneum, Ostia Antica more than rivals its sisters. Lying 25km (15 miles) southwest of Rome, its 4,000ha (10,000-acre) pastoral setting would do justice to Italy's most glorious countryside. Located on the Tiber, the port town was Rome's trade link with the outside world for 600 years—until a receding coastline and imperial decline hastened its demise. By the 17th century Ostia was all but forgotten. Legend claims its foundation in the Etruscan seventh century BC—but archaeological dating places it in the Roman fourth century BC.

From left: Detail of the remains of a Corinthian capital, preserved from the ruins and displayed at the archaeological site; the fine remnants, including the amphitheater, at this well-preserved Roman town give a good impression of what everyday life was like in an ancient port city

TOP 25

THE BASICS

ostiaantica.
beniculturali.it (online tickets)

✚ See map ▷ 114

✉ Viale dei Romagnoli 717

☎ 06 5635 0215

🕐 Apr–Aug Tue–Sun 8.30–7.15 (last admission 6.15); Nov to mid-Feb 8.30–4.30 (last admission 3.30); mid-Feb to mid-Mar 8.30–4 (last admission 3); mid-Mar to last Sat Mar 8.30–5.30 (last admission 4.30); Sep 8.30–7 (last admission 6); Oct–last Sun Oct 8.30–6.30 (last admission 5.30); closed public holidays

🍴 Restaurant

🚇 Metro line B to Piramide, then train from adjoining Roma–Lido station (covered by BIG ticket, ▷ panel 167)

🎫 Moderate; free 1st Sun of month

The site What we see today is only about half of the town, uncovered by archaeological excavations that began in the 19th century, and which continue today. Pride of place goes to the vast 4,000-seat amphitheater that is still used for open-air concerts in the summer. There are remarkable discoveries all along and leading off from the main road, Decumanus Maximus, which is rutted where laden carts once carried goods to and from the great port. Set in luxuriant greenery and surrounded by Aleppo pines and cedars are the remains of the Forum, a second-century AD multistory apartment block called the Casa di Diana, the Baths of Neptune with its splendid mosaics, and the Piazzale della Corporazione, the original business district, which is flanked by the remains of shops, offices and *horrea* (warehouses).

HIGHLIGHTS

- Aphrodite's throne
- *Galatian Soldier* statue
- Courtyard loggia
- Statue of Orestes and Electra embracing in a fond farewell

TIP

- The Palazzo Altemps is easily seen in conjunction with Piazza Navona. But note that its sister museum, the Palazzo Massimo alle Terme, is a long way away, by Termini Station.

This beautiful building epitomizes the best of Renaissance urban architecture, while its elegant rooms provide the setting for some of the finest of Rome's Classical sculpture.

The building Rome's Museo Nazionale Romano (National Roman Museum) is housed in two superbly restored buildings: the Palazzo Massimo alle Terme (▷ 40–41) near the station and here in the Palazzo Altemps, whose odd-sounding name is the Italian corruption of the German name von Hohenemps. Designed by Melozzo da Forli, and mainly constructed in the 15th century, the building houses a series of charming and intimate rooms, many with vaulted ceilings. One gives access to a splendidly frescoed loggia overlooking the comings and goings of a harmonious inner courtyard.

Clockwise from far left: The statue of Orestes and Electra; elegant rooms provide a superb backdrop for the collections; the Ludovisi Throne shows Aphrodite being plucked from the sea; statues watch over the Palazzo Altemps's peaceful inner courtyard

The best time to get a sense of the building's history is as dusk falls, when the rooms and exhibits are imaginatively lit.

The collections The palazzo is home to the Ludovisi Collection, amassed by Cardinal Ludovico Ludovisi in the 17th century, as well as the collection of Egyptian antiques and portraits. Downstairs is the *Tiber Apollo*, found in the bed of the river in the late 19th century, and two gigantic statues of Athena. Upstairs, the star of the collection, the fifth-century BC Ludovisi Throne, is probably a Greek sculpture dedicated as a throne for Aphrodite. The delicate carving portrays the goddess rising from the sea. Don't miss the statue of the *Galatian Soldier and His Wife Committing Suicide*, apparently commissioned by Julius Caesar.

THE BASICS

archeoroma.
beniculturali.it
✚ F5
✉ Piazza di Sant'
Apollinare 46
☎ 06 684851 (information) or 06 3996 7700
(ticket office); book online
at coopculture.it
🕐 Tue–Sun 9–7.45
🚌 70, 81, 87, 116T, 186,
492, 628 to Corso del
Rinascimento
💰 Moderate; combined
ticket with Palazzo
Massimo, Crypta Balbi and
Terme di Diocleziano

HIGHLIGHTS

- Scala Elicoidale
- *Madonna and Child* and *Annunciation*, Filippo Lippi
- *Holy Family* and *Madonna and Saints*, Andrea del Sarto
- *Madonna and Child*, Beccafumi
- Borromini's false-perspective window on the top floor
- *Adoration of the Shepherds* and *Baptism of Christ*, El Greco
- *Judith and Holofernes* and *Narciso*, Caravaggio
- *Beatrice Cenci*, attributed to Guido Reni
- *Henry VIII*, attributed to Holbein
- *The Triumph of Divine Providence*, Pietro da Cortona (Gran Salone)

The magnificent Palazzo Barberini—designed by Bernini, Borromini and Carlo Maderno—houses a stupendous ceiling fresco and one of Rome's finest art collections, the Galleria Nazionale d'Arte Antica.

Urban's grandeur The palace was commissioned by Maffeo Barberini for his family when he became Pope Urban VIII in 1623. It was begun by Carlo Maderno and completed by Bernini. The epitome of Rome's high baroque style, it is a maze of sumptuous suites, apartments and staircases. Overshadowing all is the Gran Salone, dominated by Pietro da Cortona's rich ceiling frescoes (1639), glorifying Urban as an agent of Divine Providence. The central windows and oval spiral staircase (Scala Elicoidale) are the work of Borromini.

Clockwise from far left: Raphael's La Fornarina forms part of the art collection; wrought-iron railings supported by decorative columns in the grounds of the palazzo; Judith and Holofernes by Caravaggio; the exterior of Palazzo Barberini; frescoes outlined in gold adorn the walls and ceiling

The collection *Antica* here means old rather than ancient. Probably the most popular painting in the collection is Raphael's *La Fornarina* (also attributed to Giulio Romano). It is reputedly a portrait of one of the artist's several mistresses, identified later as the daughter of a *fornaio* (baker). It was executed in the year of the painter's death, a demise brought on, it is said, by his mistress's unrelenting passion. Elsewhere, eminent Italian works from Filippo Lippi, Andrea del Sarto, Caravaggio and Guido Reni stand alongside paintings by leading foreign artists, such as El Greco (a *Nativity* and the *Baptism of Christ*) and Holbein (a portrait of Henry VIII, dressed for his wedding to Anne of Cleves). Also here is a splendid collection of furniture, ceramics and other beautiful examples of the decorative arts.

THE BASICS

barberinicorsini.org

🔢 J4

✉ Via delle Quattro Fontane 13

☎ 06 481 4591; book online at tosc.it

🕐 Tue–Sun 8.30–7

Ⓜ Barberini

🚌 52, 53, 58, 60, 61, 95, 116, 175, 492, 590 to Via Nazionale or Via del Tritone

♿ Few

💶 Moderate; combined ticket with Palazzo Corsini (▷ 71) moderate, valid for 3 days

TOP 25

HIGHLIGHTS

● *Religion Succored by Spain* (tagged 10), Titian
● *Portrait of Two Venetians* (23), Raphael
● *Maddalena* (40) and *Rest on the Flight into Egypt* (42), Caravaggio
● *Birth* and *Marriage of the Virgin* (174/176), Giovanni di Paolo
● *Nativity* (200), Parmigianino
● *Salomé with the Head of John the Baptist*, Titian
● Bust of Innocent X, Bernini
● *Battle of the Bay of Naples* (317), Pieter Brueghel the Elder
● *Penitent Magdalen*, Caravaggio

TIPS

● Use the audio guide, which is included in the price and helps make sense of what you're seeing.
● The paintings are not well lit so it is better to visit during daylight hours.

This is one of Rome's largest palaces and contains one of the city's finest patrician art collections. It also offers the chance to admire some of the sumptuously decorated rooms of its private apartments.

A dynasty Little in the bland exterior of the Palazzo Doria Pamphilj prepares you for the glory of the beautiful rooms that lie within. The core of the building was erected in 1435, and it has withstood countless alterations and owners. The Doria Pamphilj dynasty was formed by the union of the Doria, a famous Genoese seafaring clan, and the Pamphilj, a noble Roman family. Most people come here for the paintings, accessed through the State Apartments. These five lavish and superbly decorated saloons open out from each other

Clockwise from far left: The family chapel has an elaborate marble altar; inside, the galleries are lavishly decorated with painted ceilings and the walls adorned with ornate mirrors; Salomé with the Head of John the Baptist by Titian; a cool oasis of green—one of the palace's five inner courtyards

to reach the ballroom, with its gold and white stucco, mirrors, chandeliers and silk-hung walls. Beyond is the private chapel (1690) and the entrance to the picture galleries.

Labyrinth of masterpieces The Pamphilj's art collection is displayed in ranks in four broad galleries. As the works are numbered, not tagged, it's worth investing in a guidebook from the ticket office. The finest painting—which has a room to itself—is the famous Velázquez portrait, *Innocent X* (1650), a likeness that captured the pope's weak and suspicious nature so adroitly that Innocent is said to have lamented that it was "too true, too true." It was Innocent's nephew Camillo Pamphilj who acquired the palazzo through his marriage to Olimpia Borghese in 1647.

THE BASICS

doriapamphilj.it

✚ G5

✉ Via del Corso 305

☎ 06 679 7323

🕐 Daily 9–7 (last admission 6); plus evening concerts (expensive) when gallery can be viewed

🍴 Café-bar on ground floor

🚌 C3, 51, 62, 63, 80, 83, 85 to Via del Corso or services to Piazza Venezia

♿ Good

💰 Expensive

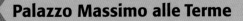

HIGHLIGHTS

● *Niobid from the Hortus Sallustiani* (Room VIII)
● The collection of coins in the basement
● *The Sleeping Hermaphrodite* (Room VII)
● House of Livia (Room II)
● *The Villa Farnesina* (Gallery II, Rooms III–V)

TIP

● The combined ticket is also valid for three days for all parts of the Museo Nazionale Romano, notably the Palazzo Altemps.

This sublime collection of Greek and Roman sculpture, with outstanding and unique displays of ancient Roman wall paintings and mosaics, dates from the end of the Republican age to the late Imperial age.

The building The Palazzo Massimo is an elegant and airy palace, beautifully renovated for the millennium. The palace, which was designed by Camillo Pistrucci, was built in the late 19th century by the Massimo family to replace an earlier one demolished to make way for Termini station. In 1981 the palace was acquired by the state, and in the 1990s it was transformed into one of Rome's most attractive museums. There are four floors of museum space, a modern library, a conference room and a computer-based documentation area.

Clockwise from far left: A pavement mosaic of the head of Pan forms part of the outstanding displays; a fourth-century BC marble inlay panel; the Lancellotti Discobolus (Discus Thrower) is among the masterpieces in the collection; intricate patterns frame this third-century BC mosaic of Dionysus

The collection This is one of two buildings (the other being the Palazzo Altemps, ▷ 34–35) housing Rome's magnificent Classical collections. Here you'll find some of the city's greatest treasures, from naked gods and games players to sarcophagi and goddesses. Don't miss the portrait busts or the wonderful Roman frescoes and mosaics on the upper floor.

Lancellotti Discobolus This fine marble copy of the great *Discus Thrower* dates from the mid-second century AD, and is one of the most famous copies of a fifth-century BC work. Discovered in the 18th century, it was sent to Germany during World War II and returned in 1948. It reproduces an original bronze that was probably the work of Myron, a Greek sculptor renowned for his portraits of athletes.

THE BASICS

archeoroma.
beniculturali.it

✚ K5

✉ Piazza dei Cinquecento 67–Largo di Villa Peretti 1

☎ Reservations 06 3996 7700 or online at coopculture.it

◷ Tue–Sun 9–7.45

🚇 Termini or Repubblica

🚌 All services to Termini and Piazza dei Cinquecento

♿ Moderate; combined ticket with Palazzo Altemps, Crypta Balbi and Terme di Diocleziano

HIGHLIGHTS

- Facade inscription
- Pedimented portico
- Original Roman doors
- Marble interior and pavement
- Coffered dome and oculus
- Tomb of Raphael
- Royal tombs

TIP

● The Pantheon is often very crowded. To make the most of your visit, go on a weekday or early in the morning.

No other monument suggests the grandeur of ancient Rome as much as this temple, whose early conversion to a place of Christian worship ensured the survival of a complete Roman imperial monument.

Temple and church The greatest surviving complete Roman structure, built by Emperor Hadrian in AD118–28, the Pantheon replaced a temple of 27BC by Marcus Agrippa, son-in-law of Augustus. (Modestly, Hadrian retained the original inscription proclaiming it as Agrippa's work.) It became the church of Santa Maria ad Martyres in AD609 (the bones of martyrs were brought here from the Catacombs) and is now a shrine to Italy's "immortals," including the artist Raphael and kings Vittore Emanuele II and Umberto I.

Clockwise from far left: Visitors gaze at the interior where massive Egyptian granite columns support the dome; the sun pours in through the oculus, an opening in the Pantheon's roof; the Pantheon borders Piazza della Rotonda and its fountain by Giacomo della Porta

An engineering marvel Massive and simple from the outside, the Pantheon is at its most breathtaking inside, where the scale, harmony and symmetry of the dome in particular are more apparent. The world's largest dome until 1882 (when it was surpassed in the English spa resort of Buxton), it has a diameter of 43.3m (142ft)—equal to its height from the floor. Weight and stresses were reduced by rows of coffers in the ceiling, and the use of progressively lighter materials from the base to the crown. The central oculus, 9m (30ft) in diameter and clearly intended to inspire meditation on the heavens above, lets light (and rain) fall onto the marble pavement far below. Relax in one of Piazza della Rotonda's cafés to enjoy and admire the exterior view of the Pantheon and the atmosphere of the piazza.

THE BASICS

- F5
- ✉ Piazza della Rotonda
- ☎ 06 6830 0230
- 🕐 Mon–Sat 9–7.30, Sun 9–6, public holidays 9–1
- 🚌 116, 119 to Piazza della Rotonda or 40, 64, 70 and all other services to Largo di Torre Argentina
- ♿ Good
- 🎫 Free

- Street market
- Statue of Giordano Bruno marking where the philosopher was martyred for heresy in 1600
- Piazza della Cancelleria
- Palazzo Pio Righetti
- Santa Maria dell'Orazione e Morte: church door decorated with stone skulls
- The inscription on "new" La Terrina (Tureen) fountain: "Do well and let them talk"

There are few places more relaxing in Rome to sit and watch the world go by than Campo de' Fiori, a lovely old piazza whose fruit, vegetable and fish market makes it one of the liveliest and most vivid corners of the old city.

Ancient square Piazza Campo de' Fiori, or the Field of Flowers, was turned in the Middle Ages from a meadow facing the ancient Theater of Pompey (55BC; now the Palazzo Pio Righetti) into one of the city's most exclusive residential and business districts. By the 15th century it was surrounded by busy inns and bordellos, some run by the infamous courtesan Vannozza Catanei, mistress of Pope Alexander VI. By February 1600 it had also become a place of execution, the fate of Giordano Bruno, a

Clockwise from far left: A selection of squashes for sale at the market; at night the bars and cafés are popular meeting places; a string of red chilies adorns a market stall; crates of fresh fruit and vegetables are transported around the market; stalls display their colorful produce

Dominican priest and philospher who was burned alive for heresy. His cowled statue stands at the center of the piazza.

Present day Just sit back and soak up the atmosphere. Students, foreigners and locals mingle with market vendors shouting their wares, while the cafés, bars and the wine bar at No. 15, the Vineria Reggio, will have you relishing the street life. One block south lies Piazza Farnese, dominated by the Palazzo Farnese, a Renaissance masterpiece partly designed by Michelangelo and begun in 1516. It is now home to the French Embassy. One block west is the Palazzo della Cancelleria (1485), once the papal chancellery. The nearby Via Giulia, Via dei Baullari, Via dei Cappellari and Via del Pellegrino are wonderful streets to explore.

THE BASICS

- F6
- Piazza Campo de' Fiori
- Market Mon–Sat 7–1.30
- 40, 46, 62, 64 to Corso Vittorio Emanuele II or C3, H, 40, 42, 62, 64, 70, 81, 87 to Largo di Torre Argentina
- Cobbled streets and some curbs around piazza
- Free

HIGHLIGHTS

- Fontana dei Quattro Fiumi (center)
- Fontana del Moro (south)
- Fontana del Nettuno (north)
- Palazzo Pamphilj
- San Luigi dei Francesi (Via Santa Giovanna d'Arco)
- Santa Maria dell'Anima (Via della Pace)

Piazza di Spagna may be more elegant and Campo de' Fiori more vivid, but Piazza Navona, with its atmospheric echoes of a 2,000-year history, is a glorious place to amble or stop for a drink at a sun-drenched table and watch the world go by.

Shaping history Piazza Navona owes its unmistakable elliptical shape to a stadium and racetrack built here in AD86 by Emperor Domitian. From the Circus Agonalis—the stadium for athletic games—comes the piazza's present name, rendered in medieval Latin as *in agone*, and then in Rome's strangulated dialect as *'n 'agona*. The stadium was used until well into the Middle Ages for festivals and competitions. The square owes its present appearance to its rebuilding by Pope Innocent X in 1644.

Clockwise from far left: Bernini's Fontana dei Quattro Fiumi is the largest fountain in Piazza Navona; the piazza at night; sculptural detail on the Fontana dei Quattro Fiumi; elegant cafés and restaurants line the square; passing the time of day beside the Fontana del Moro in the north of the square

Around the piazza Bernini's spirited Fontana dei Quattro Fiumi (Fountain of the Four Rivers) dominates. Unveiled in 1651, it has four figures that represent the four rivers of Paradise (the Nile, Ganges, Danube and Plate), and the four "corners" of the world (Africa, Asia, Europe and America). On the west side of the piazza is the baroque Sant' Agnese in Agone (1652–57), its facade designed by Borromini. Bernini's river gods are said to recoil in horror from his rival's work. Beside it stands the Palazzo Pamphilj, commissioned by Pope Innocent X and now the Brazilian Embassy. Farther afield, San Luigi dei Francesi is famous for three superlative Caravaggio paintings (in the rear chapel of the left nave), and Santa Maria della Pace for a cloister by Bramante and Raphael's frescoes of the four *Sybils*.

THE BASICS

🞡 F5

✉ Piazza Navona

🚇 Spagna

🚌 30, 70, 81, 87, 130, 492, 628 to Corso del Rinascimento or 40, 46, 62, 64 to Corso Vittorio Emanuele II

HIGHLIGHTS

- Spanish Steps
- Museo Keats-Shelley
  (▷ 70)
- Trinità dei Monti
- Fontana della Barcaccia
- Babington's Tea Rooms
- Villa Medici gardens
- Pincio gardens (▷ 72)

The Piazza di Spagna lies at the foot of the Spanish Steps, a sinuous curve rising to the Trinità dei Monti. Streams of visitors come to enjoy the views and the atmosphere.

Spanish Steps Despite their name, the Spanish Steps were commissioned by French ambassador Étienne Gueffier, who in 1723 sought to link Piazza di Spagna with the French-owned church of Trinità dei Monti on the hill above. A century earlier the piazza had housed the headquarters of the Spanish ambassador to the Holy See, hence the name of the steps and the square.

Around the steps At the base of the steps is the Fontana della Barcaccia, commissioned in 1627 by Pope Urban VIII and designed either

From left: The Fontana della Barcaccia, at the foot of the monumental staircase known as the Spanish Steps, was designed by Bernini in the shape of a small boat; enjoying the lively atmosphere in the Piazza di Spagna

by Gian Lorenzo Bernini or by his less famous father, Pietro. The eccentric design represents a half-sunken boat. As you face the steps from below, to your right stands the Museo Keats-Shelley (▷ 70), with its fascinating collection of literary memorabilia and a working library housed in the lodgings where the poet John Keats died in 1821, aged 25. At the top of the steps you can enjoy views past the magnificent Palazzo Barberini (▷ 36–37) and towards the Quirinal Hill; walk into the simple Trinità dei Monti church, with its double exterior stairs by Domenico Fontana and its frescoed chapels; and visit the beautiful gardens of the 16th-century Villa Medici, the seat of the French Academy in Rome, where French scholars come to study painting, sculpture, architecture, engraving and music.

THE BASICS

+ G4
✉ Piazza di Spagna
☎ Villa Medici 06 67611; villamedici.it. Trinità dei Monti 06 679 4179
🕐 Spanish Steps daily 24 hours. Trinità dei Monti 6.30am–8pm. Villa Medici guided visits Tue–Sun (call for latest hours and English-language tours). In English at noon
🍴 Babington's Tea Rooms
🚇 Spagna
🚌 117 to Piazza di Spagna
♿ None for Spanish Steps
🎫 Free

HIGHLIGHTS

● Choir screen
● Chapel of St. Catherine: fresco cycle
● *Ciborio* (altar canopy)
● Apse mosaic: *The Triumph of the Cross*
● Monument to Cardinal Roverella, Giovanni Dalmata (upper church)
● Fresco: *Miracle of San Clemente* (upper church)
● Fresco: *Legend of Sisinnio* (lower church)
● *Triclinium*
● Altar of Mithras: bas-relief of Mithras slaying the bull

No site in Rome reveals as vividly the layers of history that underpin the city as does this beautiful medieval ensemble. It is built over a superbly preserved fourth-century church and the atmospheric remains of a third-century Roman Mithraic temple.

The upper church The present San Clemente, which was named after Rome's fourth pope, was built between 1108 and 1184 to replace an earlier church that was sacked by the Normans in 1084. Almost untouched since, its medieval interior is dominated by the 12th-century marble panels of the choir screen and pulpits and the glittering 12th-century apse mosaic, *The Triumph of the Cross*. Equally captivating are the *Life of St. Catherine* frescoes (1428–31) by Masolino da Panicale.

Clockwise from far left: The 12th-century choir and altar in the upper church; exploring the excavated levels below the present church; detail of Masolino's Crucifixion fresco; the plain exterior of San Clemente; the decorated altar of Mithras is flanked by stone benches

Below ground Steps descend to the lower church, which retains traces of 8th- to 11th-century frescoes of San Clemente and the legends of St. Alessio and St. Sisinnio. More steps lead deeper into the twilight world of the best-preserved of the 12 Mithraic temples uncovered in Rome. (Mithraism was a popular, men-only cult that originated in Persia—modern Iran—but was later eclipsed by Christianity.) Here are an altar with a bas-relief of Mithras ritually slaying a bull, and the *triclinium*, used for banquets and rites. Ongoing excavations are revealing parts of the temple, the Mithraic schoolroom, and the 1,900-year-old remains of buildings, alleyways and streets. Even today you can hear an underground stream, which may have formed part of ancient Rome's drainage system.

THE BASICS

basilicasanclemente.com

➕ K7

✉ Via di San Giovanni in Laterano (corner of Via Labicana)

☎ 06 774 0021

🕐 Mon–Sat 9–12.30, 3–6, Sun excavations 12.15–6

🚇 Colosseo

🚌 C3, 3, 5, 51, 75, 87, 117, 118 to Piazza del Colosseo or 85, 117 to Via di San Giovanni in Laterano

♿ Church free; excavations expensive

TOP 25

HIGHLIGHTS

● The world's oldest icon of the Virgin Mary, said to be 1,000 years old, in the Pauline Chapel
● Bernini's painting *St. Cajetan Holding The Holy Child*
● The Crypt of the Nativity, with the tombs of many eminent men of the church

Santa Maria Maggiore is rightly considered Rome's finest early Christian basilica, thanks to its majestic interior and many magnificent mosaics.

History According to a myth, the Virgin appeared to Pope Liberius in his dreams on 5 August AD352, and told him to build a church exactly where snow would fall the next day. Although it was summer, snow fell, marking the outlines of a basilica on the Esquiline Hill. Legend aside, the church probably dates from AD430, though the campanile (the tallest in Rome at 75m/246ft) was added in 1377 and the interior and exterior were substantially altered in the 13th and 18th centuries. The coffered ceiling, attributed to Giuliano da Sangallo, was reputedly gilded with the first

Clockwise from far left: Santa Maria Maggiore's sublime gilded ceiling; Ferdinando Fuga's 18th-century facade and the 14th-century campanile; mosaic detail of the Coronation of the Virgin with Saints and Angels; the decorated dome of the Cappella Paolina, on the left-hand side of the nave

gold to arrive from the New World, a gift from Spain to Pope Alexander VI (note his Borgia bull emblems).

Rich decoration Beyond the general grandeur, the main treasures are the 36 mosaics in the architraves of the nave, fifth-century depictions of the lives of Moses, Abraham, Isaac and Jacob, framed by some 40 ancient columns. Also compelling are the mosaics in the loggia and on the triumphal arch. In the 13th-century apse are mosaics by Jacopo Torriti. Other highlights include the Cappella Sistina (tomb of Pope Sixtus V) by Domenico Fontana (1588); the Cappella Paolina, built by Paul V (1611); and Giovanni di Cosma's tomb of Cardinal Rodriguez (1299). The high altar reputedly contains a relic of Christ's crib.

THE BASICS

vatican.va

➕ K5

✉ Piazza di Santa Maria Maggiore and Piazza dell'Esquilino

☎ 06 6988 6800

🕐 Daily 7–6.45
Loggia and Museum: daily 9–6.30

🚇 Termini or Cavour

🚌 C3, 16, 70, 71, 75, 84, 360 to Piazza di Santa Maria Maggiore

♿ Poor: access is easiest from Piazza di Santa Maria Maggiore

🎫 Church free; Loggia and museum inexpensive

HIGHLIGHTS

● Plaques on the side of the building marking the height of the Tiber floods, which devastated the city between 1422 and 1870
● The church's star-spangled blue ceiling
● Relics of St. Catherine of Siena, and preserved room in sacristy where she died
● The headquarters of the Dominican preaching order, which serves the church, to the left of the building
● The sixth-century BC Egyptian obelisk above Bernini's elephant, known as Pulcino della Minerva (Minerva's chick)

Remarkable in having retained many Gothic features despite Rome's love for the baroque, behind its plain facade Santa Maria sopra Minerva is a cornucopia of tombs, paintings and Renaissance sculpture.

Florentine influences Originally founded in the eighth century over ruins of a temple to the Roman goddess Minerva, the church was built in 1280 to a design by two Florentine Dominican monks who fashioned it on their own church, Santa Maria Novella. Before entering the church, notice its strange but charming statue of an elephant supporting a sixth-century BC Egyptian obelisk in the pretty piazza outside. It was designed by Bernini in the 17th century. The elephant was chosen as an ancient symbol of piety and wisdom.

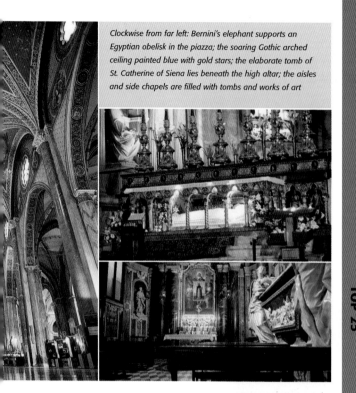

Clockwise from far left: Bernini's elephant supports an Egyptian obelisk in the piazza; the soaring Gothic arched ceiling painted blue with gold stars; the elaborate tomb of St. Catherine of Siena lies beneath the high altar; the aisles and side chapels are filled with tombs and works of art

Inside The interior of the church abounds with beautiful works, such as the Cappella Carafa (whose fine porch is attributed to Giuliano da Maiano) and Michelangelo's calm statue *The Risen Christ* (1521), left of the high altar. Filippino Lippi painted the celebrated frescoes of *St. Thomas Aquinas* and the *Assumption* (1488–93). Among other sculptures are the tombs of Francesco Tornabuoni (1480) and that of Giovanni Alberini, the latter decorated with reliefs of Hercules (15th century). Both are attributed to Mino da Fiesole. Other works include Fra Angelico's tomb slab (1455); the tombs of Medici popes Clement VII and Leo X (1536) by Antonio da Sangallo the Younger; and Bernini's monument to Maria Raggi (1643). St. Catherine of Siena, one of Italy's patron saints, is buried beneath the high altar.

THE BASICS

santamariasopra
minerva.it

🔲 G5

✉ Piazza della Minerva 42

☎ 06 6992 0384

🕐 Mon–Fri 6.40am–7pm, Sat 6.40–12.30, 3.30–7, Sun 11–6

🚌 H, 30, 40, 46, 62, 64, 70, 81, 87 to Largo di Torre Argentina

♿ Stepped access to church

🎟 Free

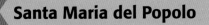
TOP 25

HIGHLIGHTS

● Cappella Costa, with the tombs of Giovanni Borgia, son of Pope Alexander VI (1492–1503), and his mother Vannozza Cattenei
● *Coronation of the Virgin*, Pinturicchio
● Cappella Cerasi with paintings by Caravaggio and Carracci
● Fresco: *Life of San Girolamo*, Tiberio d'Assisi
● *Delphic Sybil*, Pinturicchio
● Altar, Andrea Bregno
● The oldest stained-glass windows in Rome

Santa Maria del Popolo's appeal stems from its intimate size and location, and from a wonderfully varied and rich collection of works of art ranging from masterpieces by Caravaggio to some of Rome's earliest stained-glass windows.

Renaissance achievement Founded in 1099 on the site of Nero's grave, Santa Maria del Popolo was rebuilt by Pope Sixtus IV in 1472 and extended later by Bramante and Bernini. The right nave's first chapel, the Cappella della Rovere, is decorated with frescoes on the *Life of San Girolamo* (1485–90) by Tiberio d'Assisi, a pupil of Pinturicchio whose *Nativity* (c.1490) graces the chapel's main altar. The apse contains two fine stained-glass windows (1509) by the French artist, Guillaume de Marcillat.

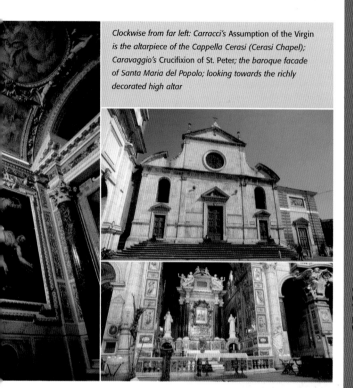

Clockwise from far left: Carracci's Assumption of the Virgin is the altarpiece of the Cappella Cerasi (Cerasi Chapel); Caravaggio's Crucifixion of St. Peter; the baroque facade of Santa Maria del Popolo; looking towards the richly decorated high altar

On either side are the greatest of the church's monuments: the tombs of the cardinals Ascanio Sforza (1505, left) and Girolamo Basso della Rovere (1507, right). Both are the work of Andrea Sansovino. High on the walls are superb and elegant frescoes (1508–10) of the *Virgin*, *Evangelists*, the *Fathers of the Church* and *Sybils* by Pinturicchio.

North nave The first chapel of the left transept, the Cappella Cerasi, contains three major paintings: the altarpiece, an *Assumption of the Virgin* by Annibale Carracci; and Caravaggio's dramatic *Conversion of St. Paul* and the *Crucifixion of St. Peter* (all 1601). The famous Cappella Chigi (1513), the second chapel in the north aisle, was commissioned by the Sienese banker, Agostino Chigi, from Raphael and Bernini.

THE BASICS

santamariadel
popolo.it

➕ F2

✉ Piazza del Popolo 12

☎ 06 361 0836

🕐 Mon–Thu 7.15–12.30, 4–7, Fri–Sat 7.30–7, Sun 7.30–1.30, 4.30–7.30

🚇 Flaminio

🚌 117 to Piazza del Popolo

♿ Few

🎟 Free

HIGHLIGHTS

● Romanesque campanile
● Facade mosaics
● Portico
● Ceiling, by Domenichino
● Cosmati marble pavement
● Wall tabernacle by Mino del Reame (central nave)
● Byzantine gold mosaics in upper and lower apse
● The nave's Roman columns; some from the Terme di Caracalla
● Madonna della Clemenza in the Cappella Altemps
● Cappella Avila: baroque chapel

TIP

● Visit in the evening, then have a drink in one of the outdoor cafés, from where you can appreciate the lit piazza and basilica.

One of the most memorable sights of nighttime Rome are the 12th-century gold mosaics on the facade of Santa Maria in Trastevere, their floodlit glow casting a gentle light over the piazza below.

Early church Santa Maria in Trastevere is among the oldest officially sanctioned places of worship in Rome. It was founded in around AD222, allegedly on the spot where a fountain of olive oil had sprung from the earth on the day of Christ's birth (symbolizing the coming of the grace of God). Much of the present church was built in the 12th century during the reign of Pope Innocent II. Inside, the main colonnade of the nave is composed of reused and ancient Roman columns. The portico, containing fragments of Roman reliefs and inscriptions, and

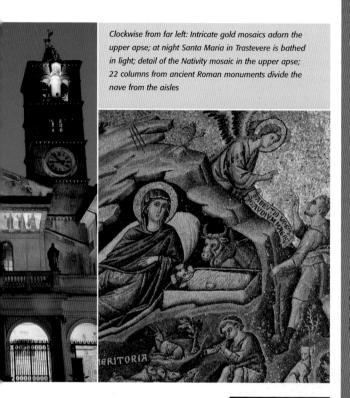

Clockwise from far left: Intricate gold mosaics adorn the upper apse; at night Santa Maria in Trastevere is bathed in light; detail of the Nativity mosaic in the upper apse; 22 columns from ancient Roman monuments divide the nave from the aisles

TOP 25

medieval remains, was added in 1702 by Carlo Fontana, who was responsible for the fountain that graces the adjoining piazza.

Mosaics The facade mosaics probably date from the mid-12th century, and depict the Virgin and Child with 10 lamp-carrying companions. Long believed to portray the parable of the Wise and Foolish Virgins, their subject matter is contested, as several "virgins" appear to be men and only two are carrying unlighted lamps (not the five of the parable). The mosaics of the upper apse inside the church, devoted to the glorification of the Virgin, date from the same period and are Byzantine-influenced works by Greek or Greek-trained craftsmen. Those below, depicting scenes from the life of the Virgin (1291), are by the mosaicist and fresco painter Pietro Cavallini.

THE BASICS

🔢 E7
✉ Piazza Santa Maria in Trastevere
☎ 06 581 4842
🕐 Daily 7.30am–9pm (may close 12.30–3.30 in winter)
🚌 H, 8, 780 to Viale di Trastevere, 125 to Via Manara or 23, 125, 280 to Lungotevere Raffaello Sanzio
♿ Wheelchair accessible
💷 Free

59

HIGHLIGHTS

● Santa Maria in Trastevere
(▷ 58–59)
● Villa Farnesina
(▷ 62–63)
● Santa Cecilia in
Trastevere (▷ 73)
● Views over Rome from
the Gianicolo
● Exploring the narrow
cobbled streets

TIP

● Visit in the evening to eat
and see the facade of Santa
Maria in Trastevere floodlit.

Picturesque Trastevere gets its name from
its location "across the Tiber." Traditionally
a working-class quarter, it is a long-
established eating and nightlife district.
Stroll the cobbled streets, browse the quirky
stores and relax in its green spaces.

Getting your bearings Viale di Trastevere
slices through the district, with a warren of narrow streets running off on either side. East lies
the ancient church of Santa Cecilia in Trastevere
(▷ 73), but Trastevere's true focus is to the
west. Amble through the alleyways to Santa
Maria in Trastevere (▷ 58–59), pausing to
take in photogenic buildings and flower-draped
restaurants. Once occupied by some of Rome's
poorest families, houses here are now snapped
up by trendy urbanites, and some crumbling

Clockwise from left: A stroll in the peaceful Orto Botanico makes a refreshing break from sightseeing; view from the Orto Botanico across Rome to Villa Medici; Piazza di Santa Maria, ringed by café terraces, is a popular meeting spot

facades hide cutting-edge designer interiors. From Santa Maria, follow Via della Scala to Villa Farnesina (▷ 62–63), set below the slopes of the Gianicolo.

Botanic garden Across the main road from the Villa lies Palazzo Corsini (▷ 71), which houses an important collection of 16th- to 17th-century art, including works by Caravaggio, Rubens and Titian. Since 1883 its gardens have been home to the Orto Botanico, Rome's botanical garden, famed for its orchid houses, herb garden, trees and old roses, and a haven in the heat. It's laid out on the lower slopes of the Gianicolo, and you can head up there for fantastic views across the city. The best are from Piazzale Garibaldi, where a huge equestrian statue commemorates the hero of Italian reunification.

THE BASICS

ortobotanicoitalia.it

➕ E8

✉ Orto Botanico, Largo Cristina di Svezia 24

☎ 06 4991 7107

🕐 Palazzo Corsini: Wed–Sat, Mon 2–7.30, Sun 8.30–7.30. Orto Botanico: Mar–Oct Mon–Sat 9–6.30; Nov–Feb 9–5.30

🍴 Vast range of cafés and restaurants

🚌 H, 8, 23, 125, 280, 630, 780

♿ Few facilities

💰 Palazzo Corsini and Orto Botanico inexpensive

HIGHLIGHTS

● Peruzzi's vibrant frescoes of trompe l'oeil views of Rome in the Sala delle Prospettive
● The gardens
● Raphael's fresco *Trionfo di Galatea (Triumph of Galatea)*

TIP

● Within the building is also the National Print Collection (Gabinetto Nazionale delle Stampe), part of the National Institute of Graphics, which can be visited by permission.

This is one of the most charming and intimate of all Rome's grand houses. It is known as much for its peaceful gardens as for its beautifully decorated interior, which contains works commissioned from Raphael and other artists by the villa's original owner, Agostino Chigi.

All to impress In 1508 Agostino Chigi, a wealthy banker from Siena, commissioned Baldassare Peruzzi to build him a suburban villa. Here, Chigi entertained artists, princes and cardinals. His banquets were memorable: after the meal, it is said that Chigi would have the gold and silver dishes thrown into the Tiber to impress his guests with his wealth. What they did not know was that the plates were caught by safety nets and returned to the kitchens.

Clockwise from far left: Visitors on a guided tour in the Sala delle Prospettive; the Villa Farnesina is set amid tranquil gardens; detail of a vibrant ceiling fresco by Peruzzi; Chigi's bedroom has an ornate ceiling and a fresco by Il Sodoma depicting the wedding night of Alexander the Great

In 1580, the villa was bought by the Farnese family, and it has been known as the Villa Farnesina ever since.

Lots to admire On the ground floor are the Loggia of Galatea, with a much-admired fresco by Raphael of the *Triumph of Galatea*, and the Loggia of Cupid and Psyche, frescoed according to Raphael's designs by some of his pupils (including the future star of Mannerist painting, Giulio Romano). On the upper floor is the beautiful Sala delle Prospettive, with a fresco by Baldassare Peruzzi of a trompe l'oeil colonnade through which can be seen rural landscapes, villages and a town. Finally, visit Chigi's former bedchamber, decorated with an erotic fresco, *The Wedding Night of Alexander the Great and Roxane*, by Il Sodoma.

THE BASICS

villafarnesina.it
🔢 E6
✉ Via della Lungara 230
☎ 06 6802 7268
🕐 Mon–Sat plus 2nd Sun of month 9–2; guided visits Mon, Fri, Sat 12.30, in English Sat 10
🚌 23, 125, 280 to Lungotevere della Farnesina
🖐 Inexpensive

More to See

This section contains other great places to visit if you have more time. Some are in the heart of the city while others are a short journey away, found under Farther Afield. This chapter also has fantastic excursions that you should set aside a whole day to visit.

MORE TO SEE

In the Heart of the City

ARCO DI COSTANTINO

Triumphal arches, like celebratory columns, were usually raised as monuments to military achievement, in this case the victory of Emperor Constantine over his imperial rival Maxentius in AD312. It was one of the last great monuments to be built in ancient Rome, and at 21m (69ft) high and 26m (85ft) wide it is also the largest of the city's arches. Most of its reliefs were taken from earlier buildings, partly out of pragmatism and partly out of a desire to link Constantine's glories with those of the past. The battle scenes of the central arch show Trajan at war with the Dacians; another describes a boar hunt and sacrifice to Apollo.

➕ J7 ✉ Piazza del Colosseo-Via di San Gregorio, Via dei Fori Imperiali 🕐 Daily 24 hours 🚇 Colosseo 🚌 C3, 30, 51, 75, 85, 87, 117, 118 to Piazza del Colosseo 🎫 Free

AVENTINO

The southernmost of Rome's seven hills is one of the city's most beautiful quarters. Here the traffic and chaos are left far behind, replaced by peaceful churches, charming cloisters, beautiful gardens and panoramic views over Trastevere and St. Peter's.

➕ G8 🚇 Circo Massimo 🚌 C3, 3, 75, 118, 628, 673 to Via del Circo Massimo

CIRCO MASSIMO

This enormous grassy arena follows the outline of a stadium once capable of seating 300,000 people. Created to satisfy the Roman appetite for chariot racing, and the prototype for almost all subsequent racecourses, it was begun around 326BC and modified frequently before the occasion of its last recorded use in AD549. Much of the original structure was robbed of its stone—old monuments were often ransacked for building materials—but the circuit's dividing wall remains, along with the ruins of the imperial box and the open arena, now a public park. Avoid after dark.

➕ H8 ✉ Via del Circo Massimo 🕐 Daily 24 hours 🚇 Circo Massimo 🚌 C3, 75, 81, 118, 160, 628, 673 to Piazza di Porta Capena 🎫 Free

Cast in evening light, the Arco di Costantino

COLONNA DI MARCO AURELIO

The Column of Marcus Aurelius (AD180–96) celebrates Aurelius's military triumphs over hostile north European tribes. It is composed of 27 separate drums of Carrara marble molded into a seamless whole, and is decorated with a continuous spiral of bas-reliefs commemorating episodes from the victorious campaigns. Aurelius is depicted no fewer than 59 times, though curiously never actually in battle. At the top of the 50m (140ft) structure stands a statue of St. Paul, which replaced the 60th depiction of Aurelius in 1589.

➕ G5 ✉ Piazza Colonna, Via del Corso
🕐 Daily 24 hours 🚇 Barberini 🚌 62, 63, 85, 95, 117 and all routes to Via del Corso
💶 Free

CRYPTA BALBI

archeoroma.beniculturali.it

This museum, part of the Museo Nazionale Romano, contains the ruins of a theater built in 13BC, along with a collection of objects to illustrate social, economic and urban planning changes from ancient times through the Middle Ages to the present day. Two other sections have displays of vases, glassware, mosaics and other items dating from between the fifth and eighth centuries.

➕ G6 ✉ Via delle Botteghe Oscure 31
📞 06 3996 7700; online booking coopculture.it 🕐 Tue–Sun 9–7.45
🚇 Colosseo 🚌 30, 40, 46, 62, 64, 70, 81, 87, 130, 190 to Largo di Torre Argentina
💶 Moderate (combined ticket)

LE DOMUS ROMANE

palazzovalentini.it

The Palazzo Valentini, a municipal office building, stands on top of the remains of some extremely upscale third-century Roman houses. These have been excavated and brought to life using every type of modern technology, giving visitors a genuine taste of prosperous life in upper-class ancient Rome. Tours take you into the houses where, through a glass floor, you see the ruins springing back to life, as frescoes

St. Paul atop the Colonna di Marco Aurelio

Fontana del Tritone, Piazza Barberini

miraculously reappear on walls, floors are laid with mosaics, and sounds and light evoke the past. It makes a wonderful introduction to the city's ruins.

🔶 H5 ✉ Palazzo Valentini, Via Foro Traiano 85 ☎ 06 2276 1280 (info and tel booking) 🕐 Wed–Mon 9.30–6.30 🚌 60, 62, 64, 85, 492 and all services to Piazza Venezia 🎫 Expensive ❓ Tickets can't be bought at the Palazzo. Either call for tickets or book online at tosc.it

FONTANA DELLE TARTARUGHE

This tiny gem of a fountain (1581–84) is one of Rome's most delightful, thanks to the four turtles, probably added by Bernini in 1658 (the current bronze sculptures are copies).

🔶 F6 ✉ Piazza Mattei 🚌 H, 8, 63, 780 to Via Arenula or 30, 70, 87 and other services to Largo di Torre Argentina

FONTANA DEL TRITONE

Like its companion piece, the Fontana delle Api, the Fontana del Tritone (1643) was also designed by Bernini for Urban VIII. One of the sculptor's earliest fountains,

the Fountain of the Triton depicts four dolphins supporting twin scallop shells bearing the Barberini coat of arms, on which the triumphant Triton is enthroned.

🔶 H4 ✉ Piazza Barberini 🚇 Barberini 🚌 C3, 53, 62, 63, 71, 80, 83, 85, 160, 492 to Piazza Barberini or Via del Tritone

FORI IMPERIALI

All five of the Imperial Fora that are featured in the Museo dei Fori Imperiali (▷ 29) stretch between the museum area and the Colosseum, and it's worth the walk to see them all. Built as political and commercial hubs by successive emperors, they have been ruthlessly plundered over time, and may seem like a haphazard collection of columns and tumbled stone, but seeing them close-up is still fascinating. Excavations are ongoing and what has been unearthed represents only half of the original fora.

🔶 H6 ✉ Via dei Fori Imperiali ☎ 06 679 7702 or 06 0608 🕐 Visible from outside only 🚇 Colosseo 🚌 51, 75, 85, 87, 117, 118 to Via dei Fori Imperiali 🎫 Free

The ruins of the Temple of Minerva, Fori Imperiali

Synagogue in the Ghetto quarter

GHETTO

museoebraico.roma.it

This picturesque place, its narrow streets full of Jewish restaurants, pastry shops and workshops, is still a meeting place for the Romano-Jewish community. The 1904 synagogue, overlooking the Tiber, houses the Jewish Museum, its dome visible from much of the city.

➕ F6 ✉ Museo: Lungotevere Cenci ☎ 06 6840 0661 🕓 Apr–Sep Sun–Thu 10–6 (last admission 5.15), Fri 10–4 (last admission 3.15); Oct–Mar Sun–Thu 10–5 (last admission 4.15), Fri 10–4 (last admission 3.15) 🚌 H, 23, 28, 63 to Lungotevere Pierleoni 🎫 Expensive (includes tour of synagogue)

ISOLA TIBERINA

This small island in the Tiber, with its medieval buildings and Roman bridges, feels like a safe haven, protected from the chaos of the city. The island is on a volcanic rock and its shape resembles that of a ship. Two bridges join it to the riverbanks: the Ponte Cestio dates back to the first century BC, and leads to Trastevere; while the Ponte Fabricio, built in 62BC, the only Roman bridge to survive intact, joins the island to the Ghetto.

➕ F7 🚌 H, 23, 63, 280, 780 to Lungotevere dei Cenci and all services to Via Arenula and Largo di Torre Argentina

MACRO

museomacro.org

Opened in 1999, this modern museum is housed in a converted brewery, with a stunning extension designed by Odile Decq. It showcases contemporary Italian art from the 1950s onwards and provides space for large-scale site-specific works and installations created by young artists.

➕ L2 ✉ Via Nizza 138 ☎ 06 6710 70400 🕓 Tue–Sun 10.30–7.30 🚌 38, 90 🎫 Expensive

MONTE PALATINO

After a stroll around the Forum it's worth climbing the Palatine Hill to enjoy this peaceful spot. Orange groves, cypresses and drowsy corners, all speckled with flowers and ancient stones, make up the Orti Farnesiani (Farnesian Gardens),

The Basilica di San Bartolomeo all'Isola, Isola Tiberina

which were laid out in the 16th century over the ruins of the palace that once stood here.

➕ H7 ✉ Entrances from Via di San Gregorio 30 and other entrances to Roman Forum ☎ 06 3996 7700 🕔 Hours as for Colosseo (▷ 19) 🚇 Colosseo 🚌 75, 87, 117 to Via dei Fori Imperiali 💶 Expensive (joint ticket valid for two days with Colosseo and Foro Romano)

MUSEO DELL'ARA PACIS
arapacis.it

Augustus's Altar of Peace, now contained within architect Richard Meier's controversial glass pavilion (opened in 2006), is decorated with bas-reliefs from 9BC. It was built to celebrate Augustus's triumphal return to Rome after campaigns in Spain and Gaul, and to commemorate the peace he had established throughout the Roman world. The outside of the enclosure is decorated with mythological scenes and grand processional friezes in which life-size figures portray Augustus, the imperial family, officials and other notables.

➕ F4 ✉ Lungotevere in Augusta, at the corner of Via Tomacelli ☎ 06 60608; online tickets at ticket.museiincomuneroma.it 🕔 Daily 9.30–7.30 🚇 Spagna 🚌 C3, 301, 628 to Piazza Augusto Imperatore or 301, 628 to Lungotevere in Augusta 💶 Expensive

MUSEO KEATS-SHELLEY
keats-shelley-house.org

Since 1909 this house, the final home of Keats and where he died in 1821 at the age of 25, has been a museum and library for students of the Romantic poets Keats and Shelley. Books, pictures and essays lie scattered around the 18th-century house.

➕ G4 ✉ Piazza di Spagna 26 ☎ 06 678 4235 🕔 Mon–Sat 10–1, 2–6 🚇 Spagna 🚌 117 to Piazza di Spagna 💶 Inexpensive

MUSEO NAZIONALE ETRUSCO DI VILLA GIULIA
villagiulia.beniculturali.it

The most important collection of Etruscan art and objects in the world is housed in a beautiful 16th-century villa. Exhibits from sites in west central and southern

A 15th-century icon painting, Museo del Palazzo di Venezia

The loggia of the Villa Giulia

Italy include Greek vases, jewelry, giant figures and tomb relics. The collection is huge, so be selective.
G1 Piazzale di Villa Giulia 9 06 322 6571; online tickets at tosc.it Tue–Sun 8.30–7.30 3, 19 Moderate

MUSEO NAZIONALE DEL PALAZZO DI VENEZIA

museopalazzovenezia.beniculturali.it
Built in 1455 for Pietro Barbo (later Pope Paul II), the former Venetian Embassy became the property of the state in 1916. There are temporary exhibitions and a permanent collection including Renaissance paintings, sculpture, armor and silverware.
G6 Palazzo Venezia, Via del Plebiscito 118 06 6999 4388; reservations 06 678 0131 Tue–Sun 8.30–7.30 All services to Piazza Venezia Moderate (inexpensive during exhibitions)

PALAZZO CORSINI

barberinicorsini.org
Though in a separate building, this gallery is part of the Palazzo Barberini's Galleria Nazionale. Originally part of the Corsini family's 17th-century collection, it became the property of the state in 1883. Pictures from the 16th to 18th centuries hang alongside bronzes and sculptures in elegant rooms.
E6 Via della Lungara 10 06 6880 2323, reservations 06 32810; tosc.it Wed–Sat, Mon 2–7.30, Sun 8.30–7.30 23, 280, 870 to Lungotevere della Farnesina Inexpensive

PALAZZO SPADA

galleriaspada.beniculturali.it
This pretty palazzo, with a creamy stucco facade (1556–62), has four rooms where you can admire the 17th- and 18th-century Spada family paintings. Cardinal Bernardino Spada is portrayed by Guido Reni; there's a fine Borromini *Perspective* and works by Albrecht Dürer, Andrea del Sarto and others.
F6 Piazza Capo di Ferro 13–Vicolo del Polverone 15b 06 32 810 or 06 683 2409 (online tickets tosc.it) Wed–Mon 8.30–7.30 H, 8, 63, 780 to Via Arenula Inexpensive

The entrance to Palazzo Corsini

A replica gilded bronze statue of Marcus Aurelius in the center of Piazza del Campidoglio

PIAZZA DEL CAMPIDOGLIO

This piazza, one of Rome's most beautiful squares, was designed by Michelangelo on the Capitoline Hill, the hub of the Roman Empire, for Emperor Charles V's triumphal entry into Rome in 1536. The buildings that stand on three sides of the square—the Palazzo Senatorio, the Palazzo Nuovo and the Palazzo dei Conservatori—were part of his scheme.

✚ G6 ✉ Piazza del Campidoglio 🚇 Colosseo 🚌 All services to Piazza Venezia

PINCIO

The park was laid out in the early 19th century. Walk to the Pincio from Piazza del Popolo or Piazza di Spagna to enjoy wonderful views (best at dusk) across the rooftops to St. Peter's.

✚ G2 ✉ Piazza del Pincio 🕐 Daily dawn–dusk 🚌 117 to Piazzale Flaminio or Piazza del Popolo 🎟 Free

SAN GIOVANNI IN LATERANO

Until the 14th century, when the popes moved to the Vatican, San Giovanni was the pontiff's seat and the focus of Christianity. It's no accident that when the fourth-century original was rebuilt in the 17th century after barbarians, earthquakes and fires destroyed it, it was modeled on St. Peter's.

✚ L8 ✉ Piazza San Giovanni in Laterano 📞 06 6988 6433 🕐 Church Apr–Sep daily 7–7; Oct–Mar 7–6/6.30. Cloisters daily 9–6; Oct–Mar 9–5. Baptistry daily 7.30–12.30, 4–6 🚇 San Giovanni 🚌 85, 117 to Piazza San Giovanni 🎟 Church free. Cloisters and baptistry inexpensive

SAN LUIGI DEI FRANCESI

The church of the French community in Rome was built between 1518 and 1589 and is devoted to St. Louis (Louis XI of France). Its Renaissance facade conceals three late masterpieces (1597–1602) by Caravaggio, all depicting episodes from the life of St. Matthew: his *Calling*, *Martyrdom*, and *Inspiration*.

✚ F5 ✉ Piazza di San Luigi dei Francesi 5 📞 06 688 271 🕐 Fri–Wed 10–12.30, 3–7, Thu 10–12.30 🚌 30, 70, 81, 87, 130, 492 to Corso del Rinascimento 🎟 Free

Inside San Giovanni in Laterano

Caravaggio's Inspiration of St. Matthew, San Luigi dei Francesi

SAN PIETRO IN VINCOLI

Rebuilt in 1475 over a basilica founded in 440, the church takes its name from the chains *(vincoli)* kept in a coffer under the high altar. It is said they are the chains used to bind St. Peter while he was held in the Mamertine prison.

🔠 J6 ✉ Piazza di San Pietro in Vincoli 4a
☎ 06 9784 4952 ⏱ Daily 8–12/12.30, 3.30–7 (Oct–Mar 3–6) 🚇 Colosseo or Cavour 🚌 75, 117 to Via Cavour or C3, 3, 51, 75, 85, 87, 117, 175 to Piazza del Colosseo 🎫 Free

SANT'AGOSTINO

One of the first Renaissance churches in Rome, Sant'Agostino still maintains its Latin Cross plan with apse, chapels and dome. It's worth visiting to see the works of Caravaggio, Raphael and other fine artists. The first chapel on the left contains Caravaggio's magnificent *Madonna di Loreto*.

🔠 F5 ✉ Piazza di Sant'Agostino ⏱ Daily 7.30–12, 4–7.30 🚌 C3, 30, 70, 81, 87 to Via Zanardelli; 30, 40, 46, 62, 63, 64, 70 and other services to Largo di Torre Argentina; 30, 70, 87 to Corso del Rinascimento

SANTA CECILIA IN TRASTEVERE

benedettinesantacecilia.it

This church is devoted to Cecilia, a young Roman woman who was martyred in the third century AD. Enter through a courtyard, with a portico supported by old granite columns and a lily garden with a central fountain. Next you pass a facade designed by Ferdinando Fuga in 1741. Crypt excavations and splendid ninth-century apse mosaics depicting Jesus with saints Paul, Agatha, Peter, Paschal, Valerian and Cecilia are among Santa Cecilia's treasures. Another is the fresco *Last Judgment* (1293) by Pietro Cavallini, the remains of a medieval masterpiece that was mostly lost in an 18th-century restoration of the church.

🔠 F8 ✉ Piazza di Santa Cecilia 22
☎ 06 589 9289 or 06 581 2140
⏱ Mon–Sat 10–12.30, 4–6, Sun 11.30–12.30, 4–6. Cavallini frescoes Mon–Sat 10–12.30. Crypt/excavations daily 10–1, 4–7 🚌 H, 8, 780 to Viale di Trastevere or Lungotevere Ripa 🎫 Church free; Cavallini fresco inexpensive; crypt inexpensive

Stefano Maderno's altar sculpture of St. Cecilia in Santa Cecilia in Trastevere (1599–1600)

Fresco of St. Benedict, Santa Maria in Aracoeli

SANTA MARIA IN ARACOELI

Perched atop the Capitoline Hill, Santa Maria in Aracoeli, with its glorious ceiling, fine frescoes and soft chandelier-lit interior, is a calm retreat from the ferocious traffic of Piazza Venezia just outside. The flight of 124 steep steps approaching Santa Maria was built in 1348 to celebrate either the end of a plague epidemic or the Holy Year proclaimed for 1350. The church is first recorded in AD574, but even then it was old. Most of the present structure, however, dates from 1260.

G6 ⊠ Piazza d'Aracoeli ☎ 06 6976 3839 🕐 May–Sep daily 9–6.30; Oct–Apr 9.30–5.30 🚌 40, 46, 62, 64, 70, 80 and all other services to Piazza Venezia 💲 Free

SANTA MARIA DELLA CONCEZIONE

cappucciniviaveneto.it

Lying in the crypt of Santa Maria della Concezione, built in 1624, are the remains of 4,000 Capuchin monks, some still dressed in jaunty clothes, the bones of others crafted into macabre chandeliers

and bizarre wall decorations. The bodies were originally buried in soil especially imported from Jerusalem. When this ran out they were left uncovered, a practice that continued until 1870.

H4 ⊠ Via Vittorio Veneto 27 ☎ 06 8880 3695 🕐 Church Mon–Sat 7–1, 3–6, Sun 9.30–12, 3.30–6. Crypt (Cimitero dei Cappuccini) daily 9–7 🚇 Barberini-Fontana Trevi 🚌 C3, 53, 61, 63, 80, 83 to Via Vittorio Veneto 💲 Moderate

SANTA MARIA IN COSMEDIN

This lovely old medieval church is best known for the Bocca della Verità (Mouth of Truth), a weather-beaten stone face (of the sea god Oceanus) once used by the ancient Romans as a drain cover. Legend claims that the mouth will clamp shut on the hands of dissemblers. Inside, the church has a beautiful floor, twin pulpits, a bishop's throne and a stone choir screen, all in fine Cosmati stone inlay. Most date from the 12th century, a little earlier than the impressive *baldacchino* (altar canopy), which was built by Deodato

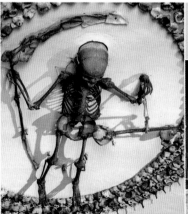

Bones in the crypt, Santa Maria della Concezione
The Bocca della Verità, Santa Maria in Cosmedin

di Cosma in 1294. In a room off the right aisle is a mosaic depicting the *Adoration of the Magi*, almost all that remains of an eighth-century Greek church on the site.

➕ G7 ✉ Piazza della Bocca della Verità 18 ☎ 06 678 7759 🕐 Apr–Oct daily 9.30–6; Nov–Mar 9.30–5 🚌 C3, 23, 81, 116, 118, 280 and other routes to Piazza Bocca della Verità or Lungotevere Pierleoni 💲 Free

TEMPIO DI VESTA AND TEMPIO DELLA FORTUNA VIRILIS

The Tempio di Vesta and Tempio della Fortuna Virilis are the two best-preserved ancient temples in Rome—all but one of the 20 columns of the former remain standing. Both date from the second century BC, the first named after its resemblance to a similar temple in the Roman Forum. The origins of the second, and the god Portunus to whom it was dedicated, remain a mystery.

➕ G7 ✉ Piazza Bocca della Verità 7 🚌 C3, H, 30, 44, 63, 80, 83, 118 and other services to Via del Teatro del Marcello and Piazza Bocca della Verità

VILLA BORGHESE

Rome's largest central park was laid out between 1613 and 1616 as the grounds of the Borghese family's summer villa. This shady retreat has walkways, woods and lakes that are complemented by an array of statues, temples and fountains, a racetrack, playgrounds and the Bioparco—a zoo and ecological center ideal for those traveling with children.

➕ H2 ✉ Porta Pinciana–Via Flaminia ☎ Bioparco 06 360 8211, bioparco.it 🕐 Daily dawn–dusk; Bioparco Apr–Oct daily 9.30–6, Nov–Mar 9.30–5 🚇 Flaminio 🚌 3, 19, 52, 53, 217, 360, 495, 910 💲 Free; Bioparco very expensive

VILLA CELIMONTANA

Set on one of the southern hills of ancient Rome and scattered with the remains of ancient buildings, this is one of the city's lesser-known parks, easily accessible from the Colosseum and San Giovanni in Laterano.

➕ J8 ✉ Piazza della Navicella 🕐 Daily 7–dusk 🚌 3 to Via del Parco del Celio or 117, 673 to Via Claudia 💲 Free

The Temple of Diana in the leafy park of Villa Borghese

Farther Afield

CATACOMBE DI SAN CALLISTO

catacombe.roma.it

These second-century catacombs are the largest and most impressive in Rome—and the most popular. They extend over 20km (12 miles) on five levels, with over 170,000 Christian burial places. You can explore claustrophobic tunnels and *loculi*, or burial niches, carved from the soft tufa stone.

➕ See map ▷ 115 ✉ Via Appia Antica 110/126 ☎ 06 513 0151 🕐 Thu–Tue 9–12, 2–5; closed Feb 🚌 714 to Piazza di San Giovanni in Laterano, then bus 218 to Fosse Ardeatine 🖐 Moderate

CATACOMBE DI SAN SEBASTIANO

catacombe.org

Above the catacombs is the fourth-century basilica, dedicated to St. Sebastian, martyred by arrows, where the saint was buried in the third century. The catacombs themselves were among the most important burial places in early Christian Rome, and may even have housed the bodies of saints Peter and Paul.

➕ See map ▷ 115 ✉ Via Appia Antica 136 ☎ 06 785 0350 🕐 Mon–Sat 10–5 (last admission 4.30); closed Dec 🚌 118, 628 to Via delle Terme di Caracalla 🖐 Moderate

MAXXI

fondazionemaxxi.it

The Museo Nazionale delle Arti del XXI Secolo, an extraordinary gallery of 21st-century art, is the work of architect Zaha Hadid. It includes work from the last 40 years as well as cutting-edge contemporary Italian and international art.

➕ See map ▷ 114 ✉ Via Guido Reni 4a ☎ 06 320 1954 🕐 Tue–Fri, Sun 11–7, Sat 11–10 🚇 Line A to Flaminio then tram 2 🚌 53, 168, 280, 910 🖐 Expensive; free to Gallery 4 Tue–Fri and last Sun of month

MONTE GIANICOLO

The best view of Rome is from the Janiculum Hill. There are views all the way up from the Passeggiata del Gianicolo, an avenue that runs around the hill. En route visit the little Tempietto designed by Bramante in 1508, and the church of San Pietro in Montorio.

The view from the Gianicolo

Zaha Hadid's remarkable MAXXI gallery of modern art

MORE TO SEE

D7 ✉ Passeggiata del Gianicolo
🕐 Tempietto Via Garibaldi 33: Tue–Sun
10–6; church Mon–Fri 8.30–12, 3–4, Sat,
Sun 8.30–12 🚌 115, 125, 870 to the
Gianicolo or Via Garibaldi 💶 Church and
Tempietto free

SAN PAOLO FUORI LE MURA

basilicasanpaolo.org

The church of St. Paul outside the
Walls marks the spot where St.
Paul was buried after his execution
in AD67. Begun in AD385, it
replaced several smaller churches
on the site. It was one of the city's
most richly decorated buildings,
but a fire in 1823 destroyed the
church and most of its treasures.
Much of the vast church you see
today dates from the 19th century,
though one or two artistic masterpieces survived the fire, notably a
beautiful altar canopy by Arnolfo di
Cambio dating from 1285.

🗺 See map ▷ 114 ✉ Piazzale San Paolo
1, Via Ostiense 186 ☎ 06 6988 0800/0802
🕐 Daily 7–6.30 (5.30 in winter) 🚇 Line B
to Basilica di San Paolo 🚌 23 to Ostiense/
LGT San Paolo or 271 to Viale di San Paolo
💶 Church free

TERME DI CARACALLA

archeorm.arti.beniculturali.it

Ancient Rome's luxurious baths
could hold as many as 1,600
bathers. Started by Septimius
Severus in AD206, and completed
11 years later by his son, Caracalla,
they were designed for gatherings
as well as for hygiene. The site is
now a venue for outdoor opera
and concerts.

🗺 J9 ✉ Via delle Terme di Caracalla 52
☎ 06 575 8626; online tickets at
coopculture.it 🕐 Tue–Sun 9–1 hour before
sunset, Mon 8.30–2; closed public holidays
🚇 Circo Massimo 🚌 C3, 75, 81, 118, 160,
628 to Via di San Gregorio-Via delle Terme
di Caracalla 💶 Moderate (combined
L'Archaeologia card gives admission to
tombs on Via Appia)

VILLA DORIA PAMPHILJ

If you fancy a long walk away from
the crowds, there's nowhere better
than here in Rome's largest public
landscaped park. Jogging and
cycling are popular activities.

🗺 B8 ✉ Via di San Pancrazio 🕐 Daily
dawn–dusk 🚌 115, 125, 870 to the
Gianicolo or Via Garibaldi

*San Paolo Fuori le Mura's apse mosaic
depicting Christ flanked by the Apostles*

Ancient Rome's public baths, Terme di Caracalla

Excursions

FRASCATI

Frascati is the loveliest of the Castelli Romani, 13 towns in the Colli Albani, south of Rome, so-called because they grew up around the feudal castles of the city's popes and patrician families. The Colli Albani are 60km (37 miles) of volcanic hills, known for their wine, lakes, pretty countryside and—above all—as a refuge from the summer heat of Rome.

Many of the Castelli were badly damaged during fighting in 1944 and have a number of modern buildings. Frascati, however, retains much of its charm, and is also the easiest town to reach from central Rome. Come by train and you are rewarded with an appealing ride through some of the Roman Campagna (countryside) as the line climbs into the hills.

The chances are that if you drink house white wine in Rome's restaurants it will come from Frascati, or near by, but the locals say it is best drunk *sul posto* (on the spot). There are any number of cafés and *fraschette* (taverns)

dotted around the pedestrian-only old quarter—one of the most historic is the Grappolo d'Oro at Piazza Fabio Filzi 5; or visit the stalls in Piazza del Mercato.

The grandest of Frascati's villas is the Villa Aldobrandini, above Piazza Marconi. It was designed in 1598 by Giacomo della Porta for Cardinal Aldobrandini, a nephew of Pope Clement VII. The great villa itself, all faded majesty, is rarely open, but visits are generally possible to the wonderful baroque garden. Don't miss the sweeping views from the main front terrace.

Elsewhere, visit the cathedral, the church of Il Gesù, and the town park, formerly the gardens of the Villa Torlonia, which was destroyed in 1944.

Distance: 20km (12 miles)
Journey time: 30–40 min
🚆 Train from Termini 🚌 COTRAL bus from Anagnina metro station
Villa Aldobrandini
✉ Via Cardinale Massaia 18 ☎ 06 683 3785 🕐 Garden only Apr–Nov Mon–Fri 9–1, 3–6; Dec–Mar Mon–Fri 9–1, 3–4 💶 Moderate

Views of the countryside around Frascati

The terraces at Villa Aldobrandini are decorated with statues

TIVOLI

Tivoli is one of the most popular excursions from Rome, thanks to the town's lovely wooded position on a bend of the River Aniene, the superlative gardens of the Villa d'Este and the ruins and grounds of Hadrian's Roman villa. It can be busy, especially at weekends, so arrive early to see everything.

The Este gardens were laid out in 1550 as part of a country retreat for Cardinal Ippolito d'Este, son of Lucrezia Borgia and the Duke of Ferrara. Highlights among the beautiful terraces and fountains are the Fontana dell'Organo (Organ Fountain), which plays tunes, and the Fontana della Civetta (Owl Fountain), which spouts birdsong.

Also worth seeing is the Villa Gregoriana, a more unkempt park created in 1831. Explore the paths through the park's gorge for some fine views of the luxuriant vegetation and two crashing waterfalls.

The Villa Adriana requires a trip out of town but it is well worth it for its romantic classical ruins. The largest villa discovered in the Roman Empire, it was built between AD118 and AD135 as a retirement home for Emperor Hadrian and covered an area greater than the center of Rome.

Distance: 31km (19 miles)

Journey time: 1 hour

🚆 Train from Termini 🚇 Metro line B to Ponte Mammolo and then COTRAL bus to Tivoli in direction Via Prenestina

Villa d'Este

villadestetivoli.info

✉ Piazza Trento ☎ 199 766 166; online booking at vivaticket.it 🕐 Tue–Sun 8.30–1 hour before dusk; last admission 90 min before closing 💰 Moderate

Villa Gregoriana

visitfai.it/parcovillagregoriana

✉ Piazza Tempio di Vesta and Largo Sant' Angelo ☎ 0774 332650 🕐 Apr–Sep Tue–Sun 10–6.30; Mar, Oct to mid-Dec 10–4 (closed rest of 2017) 💰 Moderate

Villa Adriana

villaadriana.beniculturali.it

✉ Via di Villa Adriana-Via Tiburtina ☎ 06 3996 7900 (online tickets at coopculture.it 🕐 Daily 9–1 hour before dusk 🚌 CAT shuttle bus 4 or 4X from Tivoli centre 💰 Moderate

The Organ Fountain in the grounds of the Villa d'Este

City Tours

This section contains self-guided tours that will help you explore the sights in each of the city's regions. Each tour is designed to take a day, with a map pinpointing the recommended places along the way. There is a quick reference guide at the end of each tour, listing everything you need in that region, so you know exactly what's close by.

CITY TOURS

The Ancient City

Ancient monuments can be found across present-day Rome, but the heart of the ancient city centers on an area containing the Roman Forum, the Colosseum and several other majestic ruins, along with magnificent churches and grand museums.

Morning
Start your day in **Piazza Venezia** and admire the **Monumento a Vittorio Emanuele II**, the vast white edifice that dominates this big and busy square. Then climb the ramp, designed by Michelangelo, to **Piazza del Campidoglio** (▷ 72) and pay a quick visit to **Santa Maria in Aracoeli** (▷ 74). Exit the piazza down the lane in its far left corner for a lovely overview of the Roman Forum before descending to Via dei Fori Imperiali to look at the **Fori Imperiali** (▷ 68), located below street level either side of the road. Then allow a good hour or two to explore the **Foro Romano** itself (▷ 22–23).

Mid-morning
The Forum has little shade, so towards the end of your visit climb the slopes of **Monte Palatino** (▷ 69–70) for a break in its shady gardens. Your Forum ticket is valid for the Palatine and for the **Colosseo** (▷ 18–19), which you should visit next—exit the Forum beyond the Arco di Tito and the amphitheater is in front of you. Don't overlook the **Arco di Costantino** (▷ 66), on your right just after you exit the Forum, and be sure to join the correct ticket-holders' line for the Colosseum.

Lunch
Check your watch and, if it's still open, visit **San Pietro in Vincoli** (▷ 73), barely five minutes' walk from the Colosseum. For lunch, avoid the generally poor-quality cafés in Piazza del Colosseo and walk a few minutes to one of the evening choices (see facing page). Alternatively, you can eat a picnic in the nearby **Parco di Traiano**.

Afternoon

If you like churches, now is the time to visit **San Giovanni in Laterano** (▷ 72), which is open all day. If you want less of a walk, and a more manageable and fascinating church, restrict yourself to **San Clemente** (▷ 50–51), but note that it does not usually open until mid-afternoon.

Mid-afternoon

Retrace your steps to Piazza del Campidoglio and perhaps take a break on the terrace café of the Monumento a Vittorio Emanuele II, which has good views of the **Fori Imperiali** (▷ 68). If you still have the energy for a museum, see the **Musei Capitolini** (▷ 24–25). If the **Mercati di Traiano** (▷ 28–29) or **Le Domus Romane** (▷ 67) sound more appealing, they are both within a short walk of Piazza Venezia, just down the steps from the Capitoline.

Evening

It is well worth returning here at night, or remaining here at the end of your day, to enjoy the sight of several floodlit monuments, especially the **Colosseo** (▷ 18–19) and **Piazza del Campidoglio** (▷ 72). Climb the steps or take the escalator to the terrace (Largo G. Agnesi) above the Colosseo metro station for an especially good view of the amphitheater. If it's early and you just want a snack or light meal, try the **Oppio Caffè** (▷ 136) in the Parco di Traiano; for a fuller meal, the grid of streets east of the Colosseum has several choices, including **Pasqualino** (▷ 149) and **Il Bocconcino** (▷ 144), which both serve good traditional food.

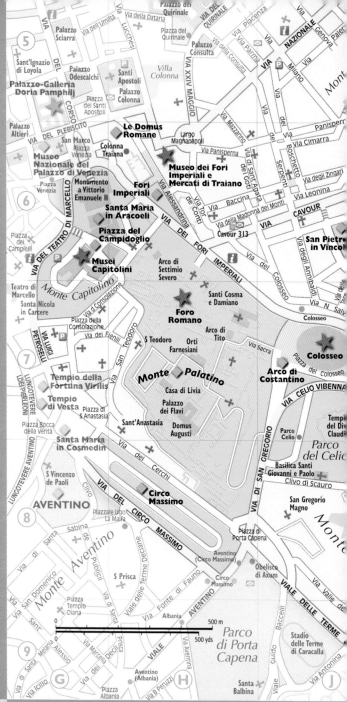

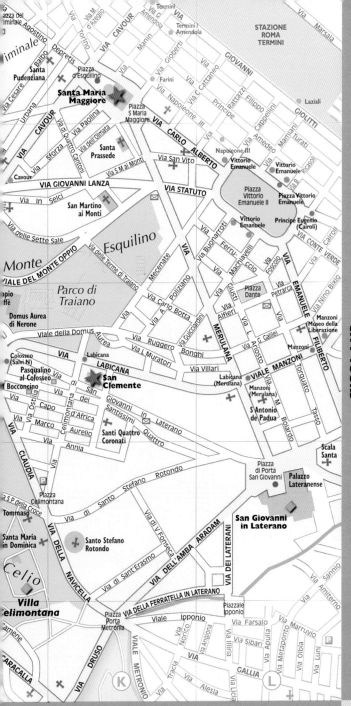

SIGHTS AND EXPERIENCES

CITY TOURS

Colosseo (▷ 18)
The Colosseum is the greatest surviving monument from Roman antiquity, a huge amphitheater built in the first century AD to stage gladiatorial combats and games.

Foro Romano (▷ 22)
Ruins in the Roman Forum span almost 1,500 years, the legacy of an era when this was the political, social, religious and administrative hub of the Roman Empire.

Musei Capitolini (▷ 24)
These two museums on the Capitoline Hill contain Roman and Greek masterpieces, as well as an outstanding collection of Renaissance and other paintings.

Museo dei Fori Imperiali e Mercati di Traiano (▷ 28)
Once the Foro Romano became too cramped, successive emperors created new imperial fora, including Trajan's market complex.

San Clemente (▷ 50)
Three places of worship make up this multi-level complex: a medieval church, an earlier church below and an ancient Roman Mithraic temple below that.

Santa Maria Maggiore (▷ 52)
This fourth-century basilica is one of the great churches of Rome, its vast interior graced with lavishly decorated chapels, and fifth-century mosaics in the nave.

CITY TOURS

87

Central Rome

Central Rome embraces the medieval, Renaissance and baroque heart of the city, offering a superb variety of palaces, churches, galleries, shops, markets, restaurants and cafés, cobbled streets and fountain-filled piazzas.

Morning
Join the market traders early for a cappuccino in **Piazza Campo de' Fiori** (▷ 44–45), being sure to walk into the adjoining **Piazza Farnese** to admire its fountains and the **Palazzo Farnese**. If the small **Palazzo Spada** gallery (▷ 71) appeals, now is the time to see it. Then make your way to the **Pantheon** (▷ 42–43) via Largo di Torre Argentina, Via dei Cestari (known for its shops selling ecclesiastical wear) and **Santa Maria sopra Minerva** (▷ 54–55). From the Pantheon walk to **Piazza Navona** (▷ 46–47) via **San Luigi dei Francesi** (▷ 72), and perhaps pop into **Sant'Agostino** (▷ 73), just north of the square, before it closes around midday.

Mid-morning
Cafés on and around Piazza Navona are often expensive, especially if you sit outside, but it's worth paying over the odds to enjoy the lovely setting. Away from the square, **Bar del Fico** (▷ 143) is a simple locals' place. So, too, are **La Tazza d'Oro** (▷ 151) and **Sant'Eustachio** (▷ 150) nearer the Pantheon, not so much for their setting but because both claim to offer Rome's best cup of coffee.

Lunch
Before lunch, devote an hour or so to exploring the picturesque streets west of **Piazza Navona**, many of which contain interesting shops and plenty of options for a light lunch. Via del Governo Vecchio, Via dei Coronari and Via dei Banchi Nuovi are especially good, as are Via dei Banchi Vecchi, Via Giulia and Via dei Cappellari west of Piazza Campo de' Fiori.

Afternoon

The afternoon can be devoted to two galleries, with relatively small but superb collections of contrasting exhibits: the Roman sculptures of the **Palazzo Altemps** (▷ 34–35), which is open all day and is a short walk north of Piazza Navona, and the paintings of the **Palazzo-Galleria Doria Pamphilj** (▷ 38–39). Walk between the two via Piazza di Montecitorio and the **Colonna di Marco Aurelio** (▷ 67).

Evening

The area around **Piazza Navona** is one of the city's main restaurant districts, so there are plenty of options (not all good) in the narrow, medieval streets, many of which are lined with tables spilling onto the cobbles on summer evenings. Even if you don't eat or drink here, it's a wonderful, bustling area to walk around. Piazza Navona is a natural meeting place, as is **Piazza della Rotonda** in front of the **Pantheon**. Finish the evening with an ice cream from **Tre Scalini** (▷ 151) or **Gelateria della Palma** (▷ 147).

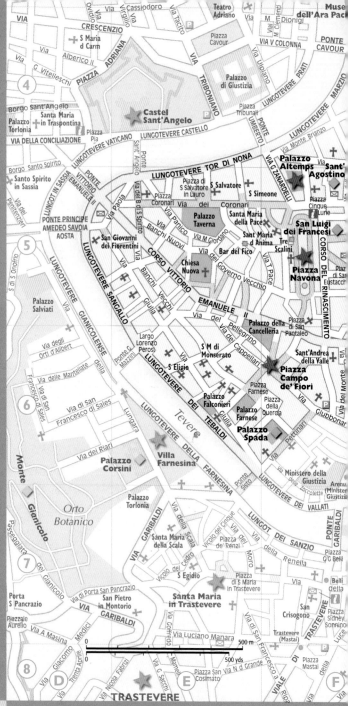

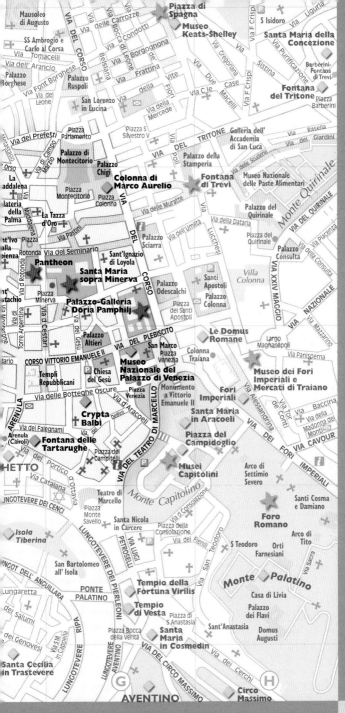

SIGHTS AND EXPERIENCES

CITY TOURS

Palazzo Altemps (▷ 34)
This exquisite Renaissance palace plays host to some of the greatest of all Roman sculptures, among them Aphrodite's throne.

Palazzo-Galleria Doria Pamphilj (▷ 38)
This vast palace has over 1,000 rooms and is home to a priceless collection of Italian art.

Pantheon (▷ 42)
Emperor Hadrian's temple is the world's best-preserved Roman monument, with an awe-inspiring entrance and a beautiful interior.

Piazza Campo de' Fiori (▷ 44)
The "Field of Flowers" is ringed with cafés and bars and holds a lively and colorful traditional food and flower market.

Piazza Navona (▷ 46)
Rome's most elegant piazza contains a church and fountains designed by baroque architects, Bernini and Borromini.

Santa Maria sopra Minerva (▷ 54)
Discover a statue by Michelangelo and a sublime Renaissance fresco cycle in this lovely Gothic church.

MORE TO SEE	64

Colonna di Marco Aurelio
Crypta Balbi
Fontana delle Tartarughe
Museo Nazionale del Palazzo
  Venezia

Palazzo Spada
San Luigi dei Francesi
Sant'Agostino

Trastevere and the South

The former Ghetto and picturesque Trastevere area are more traditional quarters, full of narrow streets, local markets and neighborhood bars and restaurants.

Morning
Start at **Santa Maria in Cosmedin** (▷ 74), where you could try putting your hand in the Bocca della Verità in the porch—legend says that liars will get a hearty bite. Cross the road to admire the **Tempio di Vesta** and the **Tempio della Fortuna Virilis** (▷ 75) and then cut down to walk along the Lungotevere dei Pierleoni beside the river, with the Isola Tiberina ahead in the water. This will bring you to the end of Via Portico d'Ottavia, named for the ruins of a Roman gateway that stands here. It was built as part of a massive complex by Emperor Augustus in the first century BC and dedicated to his sister, Octavia. Today it forms part of the church of **Sant'Angelo in Pescheria**, to its left, which takes its name from the fish market that flourished on the site from Roman times until the Middle Ages.

Mid-morning
Explore the pretty labyrinth of little streets north of the Portico, then return to Via Portico d'Ottavia and follow it left and south past the Teatro di Marcello to the river and the synagogue and its **museum** (▷ 69). Cross the Ponte Fabricio in front of you and walk around the **Isola Tiberina** (▷ 69), with a visit (if open) to the church of **San Bartolomeo**. Cross the Ponte Cestio to the Trastevere area. Not far from the bridge is the church of **Santa Cecilia in Trastevere** (▷ 73).

Lunch
The most attractive part of Trastevere, and the area with the best choice of places for lunch, lies on the west side of Viale di Trastevere. You may want to eat here this evening, so consider a café snack or buy a picnic, perhaps from the stalls of the market in Piazza di San Cosimato.

CITY TOURS

Afternoon

Sometimes **Santa Maria in Trastevere** (▷ 58–59) is open all day; sometimes it closes for a period between around 1 and 3. If it is still shut when you have finished lunch, explore some of the streets nearby, then see the church. Afterwards, walk down Via della Scala and Via della Lungara to see the **Villa Farnesina** (▷ 62–63). If time allows, see nearby **Palazzo Corsini** (▷ 71) and/or take a break in the **Orto Botanico** (▷ 61).

Evening

Trastevere comes alive in the evenings, especially on and around Piazza di Santa Maria in Trastevere. Admire the floodlit mosaics on the facade of Santa Maria di Trastevere; enjoy the street life in the small lanes nearby; and perhaps take a drink in the earthy **Bar San Calisto** (▷ 133).

Dinner

Trastevere has many traditional-style restaurants, such as the refined **Paris** (▷ 149; reserve ahead), as well as a plethora of *pizzerie*, of which **Ivo** (▷ 148) and **Dar Poeta** (▷ 146) are classic examples. But it also has a new breed of contemporary dining options, such as **Glass Hosteria** (▷ 148), many of which are gathered around Piazza Trilussa.

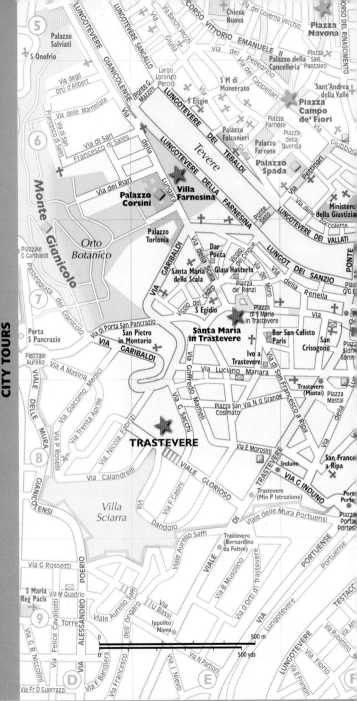

SIGHTS AND EXPERIENCES

Santa Maria in Trastevere (▷ 58)

In a neighborhood of narrow streets, the 12th- to 13th-century church, with a Romanesque bell tower and mosaic-filled facade, and its square (Piazza Santa Maria in Trastevere) stand out. Both are especially lovely at night, when they are floodlit. The interior of the church is lined with Roman columns and baroque chapels under a sumptuous painted ceiling and a series of glittering mosaics.

Trastevere (▷ 60)

Trastevere means "across the Tiber" and you can cross a genuine Roman bridge, the Ponte Cestio, to reach this beguiling area. Once a blue-collar enclave, today it is a maze of picturesque streets, houses, bars, restaurants and quirky one-off stores, while its must-see sights include ancient churches such as Santa Maria in Trastevere, the Renaissance Villa Farnesina and the botanic garden.

Villa Farnesina (▷ 62)

Trastevere, for the most part, has historically been a poorer area of the city. Most of Rome's great palaces were built elsewhere. The Villa Farnesina is an exception, originally created for a Tuscan banker and later bought by the powerful Farnese family. More intimate than its neighbors across the river, it is best known for its lovely interior decoration, and for the frescoes designed and painted by Raphael and Baldassare Peruzzi.

CITY TOURS

Northern Rome

Northern Rome embraces historic and more recent areas of the city, as well as landmark sights such as Piazza di Spagna and the Fontana di Trevi, along with central Rome's principal park and several of its major galleries.

Morning

Most of northern Rome's sights are too far away and too widely separated to see in a single, coherent itinerary. Four are also major galleries, two of which are probably enough for one day. If the Etruscans appeal, take a taxi to and from the **Villa Giulia** (▷ 70–71) and make this a self-contained visit. The same goes for the **Museo e Galleria Borghese** (▷ 30–31), though here you could walk back towards the city center through the **Villa Borghese** (▷ 75) and via the **Pincio** gardens (▷ 72) to Piazza del Popolo (to see **Santa Maria del Popolo**, ▷ 56–57) and from there along to **Piazza di Spagna** (▷ 48–49) on Via Margutta or Via del Babuino.

Mid-morning

Alternatively, you could walk from the Museo directly to **Piazza di Spagna** (▷ 48–49), descending the Spanish Steps, where you'll find the **Museo Keats-Shelley** (▷ 70). This is another museum, but a small one, and its displays—devoted to the English Romantic poets and their circle—are in marked contrast to other galleries and museums of Roman, medieval or Renaissance art and sculpture in the area. If the museum does not appeal, take a break in one of the cafés on or near Piazza di Spagna or explore the many chic shops in the grid of streets around Via Condotti.

Lunch

Restaurants around Piazza di Spagna and Via Condotti tend to be expensive. You'll find better value and more choice west of **Via del Corso**, a slightly less exclusive shopping street. Better still, walk up Via Margutta, where you could eat fresh vegetarian food at **Margutta RistorArte** (▷ 148). Alternatively, there are other choices along Via del Babuino and cafés for a snack lunch in **Piazza del Popolo**.

Afternoon

If you have lunched near Piazza del Popolo, then you'll be well placed to see the controversial **Museo dell'Ara Pacis** (▷ 70). This will leave you slightly out on a limb, however, and you might prefer to make straight for the **Fontana di Trevi** (▷ 20–21), but be prepared for the crowds that throng the fountain day and night. You are now reasonably close to the spooky **Santa Maria della Concezione** (▷ 74) and **Palazzo Barberini** (▷ 36–37), but if you have already seen the Museo e Galleria Borghese, note that the art in the latter is from a similar period.

Mid-afternoon

Instead, consider the Roman collection of the **Palazzo Massimo alle Terme** (▷ 40–41), but take a bus or a taxi from Via del Tritone, as the walk—unless you wend through the back streets between Via del Quirinale and Via Nazionale—is unappealing. The museum is close to Termini station for buses or taxis back to your hotel.

Evening

At the end of a summer's day, there are few nicer places for a pre-dinner drink than the **Stravinskij Bar** (▷ 137), with its lovely courtyard garden. A few minutes' walk would then take you to **Matricianella** (▷ 149) for dinner, a restaurant that is well placed for a stroll after eating to admire the floodlit Trevi Fountain or to buy an ice cream at **Il Gelato di San Crispino** (▷ 147), not far from the famous fountain.

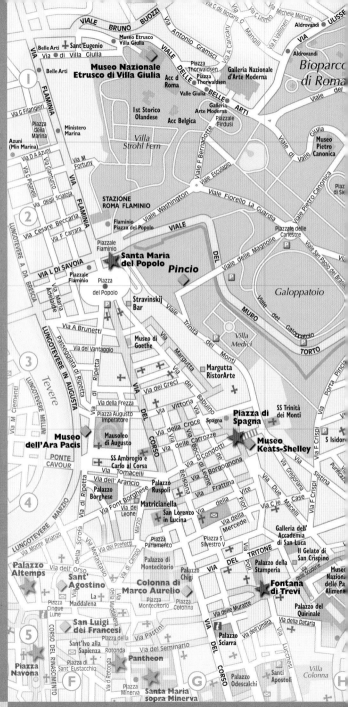

Bioparco

Pza
Giuseppe
Verdi

Istituto Poligrafico
e Zecca dello Stato

VIALE

Via Rubicone

Piazza
Mincio

ALDROVANDI

Via Carissimi

Via G B Martini

VIALE

REGINA

Via
Arno
Via Tanaro

Via Aremo

useo Civico
Zoologica

Via N
Ponora

Via G Giovannelli

SCARLATTI

Via Arno

Buenos
Aires

Via Ombrone

iardino
Zoologico

Mercadante

Via Pietro Raimondi

Donizetti

Via C Pacini

Via Mercuro

Via Tirso

MARCHERITA

Parco dei
Daini

PAISIELLO

Via N

Via R Giovannelli

Po

Simeto

Basento

Via del
Uccelliera

Via C Allegri

Via J Peri

Adda

Villa
Albani

Museo e
Galleria
Borghese

PINCIANA

Savoia

SALARIO

Piazzale
dei Cavalli
Marini

Cavalli

Via Museo Borghese

Via Marini

Via

Via Livenza

SALARIA

Via di Villa Albani

Museo d'Arte
Contemporanea
MACRO

Villa
Borghese

Po

Isonzo

Via Velletri

Via Nizza

Via Brescia

Via
Messina

oethe

Viale del

PINCIANA

Via d S Teresa

Via Sesia

S Teresa

Via Bergamo

Piazza
Alessandria

Via Ancona

CORSO

D'ITALIA

CORSO

D'ITALIA

Campania

Piazzale
Porta Pia

VIA VITTORIO VENETO

Sardegna

Via Puglie

Via Lucania

Via A Valenziani

Villa
Paolina

Ministero delle
Infrastrutture
e dei Trasporti

Via

Abruzzi

Sicilia

S S Redent

Porta
Pia

Lazio

Via Marche

Via Toscana

Via

BONCOMPAGNI

Piemonte

Via Quintino Sella

Via Collina

VIA

Emilia

ombardia

Friuli

Lucullo

Sallustiana

Via

Flavia

SETTEMBRE

Via Goito

PALESTRO

Ludovisi

Via G Carducci

Aureliana

XX

Liguria

Via Antonio
Salandra

Ministero
dell'Economia
e delle Finanze

CERNAIA

Via Montebello

Castelfidardo

VITTORIO VENETO

VIA L BISSOLATI

Ministero delle politiche
agricole alimentari
e forestali

VIA

Via

Via Gaeta

Santa Maria della
Concezione

Via S Basilio

Via S N da Tolentino

BARBERINI

Santa Maria
della Vittoria

Via Parigi

Via Volturno

Piazza
Indipendenza

zza
berini

Barberini-
Fontana di Trevi

Via S N da Tolentino

EMANUELE ORLANDO

VIA BARBIERI

Terme di
Diocleziano

Via Marsala

Fontana
el Tritone

Palazzo
Barberini

SETTEMBRE

Via Firenze

Repubblica-
Teatro dell'
Opera

Santa Maria
degli Angeli

VIALE ENRICO DE NICOLA

VIA GIOVANNI GIOLITTI

aselia

XX

Ministero
della Difesa

Piazza della
Repubblica

VIALE EINAUDI

Piazza dei
Cinquecento

STAZIONE
ROMA
TERMINI

Giardini

VIA DELLE QUATTRO FONTANE

San Carlo alle
Quattro Fontane

Via delle Quattro Fontane

Via Firenze

Via Modena

Via Torino

Palazzo
Massimo
alle Terme

Termini

Monte

Quirinale

Sant'Andrea
del Quirinale

NAZIONALE

Teatro dell'
Opera

Viminale

VIA CAVOUR

Termini /
Amendola

Via C Amendola

Via Placenza

Via Genova

Piazza del
Viminale

Via Firenze

Via Napoli

Via Agostino Depretis

Santa
Pudenziana

Piazza
d'Esquilino

Via Principe

Via Amedeo

nella Consulta

Via Milano

Ist
Chimico

Via Cesare

Balbo

J

Santa Maria
Maggiore

K

Farini

500 m

500 yds

103

SIGHTS AND EXPERIENCES

Fontana di Trevi (▷ 20)

Throw a coin into Rome's prettiest and most famous fountain and legend says that you will be sure to return to the city.

Museo e Galleria Borghese (▷ 30)

You need to pre-book your visit to enjoy the beauty of the Borghese palace, its paintings and sculptures.

Palazzo Barberini (▷ 36)

Paintings by Caravaggio and Raphael form part of the collection of art and antiquities in this lavishly decorated baroque palace.

Palazzo Massimo alle Terme (▷ 40)

A fine setting for some of the city's best Roman and Greek frescoes, murals and sculpture.

Piazza di Spagna (▷ 48)

The Piazza di Spagna is the setting for one of Rome's great sights, the Spanish Steps, and the focus of the city's luxury shopping district.

Santa Maria del Popolo (▷ 56)

One of Rome's most atmospheric small churches, with sculptures by Jacopo Sansovino and paintings by Pinturicchio and Caravaggio.

CITY TOURS

Vatican and Around

Vatican City is an independent state that is home to St. Peter's and the Vatican Museums, a vast complex that contains the Sistine Chapel. Close by is the Castel Sant'Angelo, whose long history has seen it used as a mausoleum, fortress, prison and museum.

Morning
Lines for the **Musei Vaticani** (▷ 26–27) can be extremely long, whatever the time of year, so arrive as early as possible, or preferably book ahead online. You will probably need most of the morning simply to see the highlights of the various museums, but note that you will not be allowed to spend long in the **Cappella Sistina**—such is the weight of people wanting to see Michelangelo's famous frescoes that visitors are constantly kept on the move.

Mid-morning
The museums have a café if you wish to take a break from the more than 11km (7 miles) of galleries that make up the complex.

Lunch
Exit the museums and turn right down the hill to Piazza del Risorgimento, which has a selection of mediocre cafés and pizzerias. Better options are to the north (try **Dal Toscano**, ▷ 146, in Via Germanico) or head towards the Ottaviano metro station; there are some good choices along here, including **Pizzarium Bonci** (▷ 150) and **La Pratolina** (▷ 150). Restaurants in this area are likely to be busy.

Afternoon
It is an easy walk from the Musei Vaticani to Piazza San Pietro and the **Basilica di San Pietro** (▷ 14–15). You will have to stand in line on the northwest side of the piazza for a security screening before entering the basilica. Lines are shorter later in the afternoon, but note that the church usually closes at 7pm or earlier. This said, you probably won't need to spend more than an hour in the church unless you wish to climb the dome. This leaves time to visit the **Castel Sant'Angelo** (▷ 16–17), a walk along Via della Conciliazione. If you didn't want to see the Vatican Museums, a straightforward alternative itinerary might see you visiting the Castel early in the morning and the basilica before lunch.

Evening
You should make an effort to linger in—or return to—**Piazza San Pietro** in the evening to enjoy the piazza and the basilica under floodlights. The area does not have as many good dining possibilities as the rest of central Rome, but you can enjoy a light and elegant meal with a superb wine at **Del Frate** (▷ 146). Or, if you didn't stop there for lunch, head for **La Pratolina** (▷ 150), a great choice for sampling some very special pizza and generally buzzing with Romans and visitors.

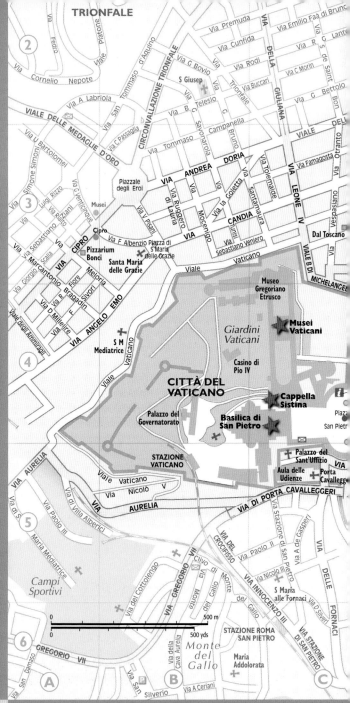

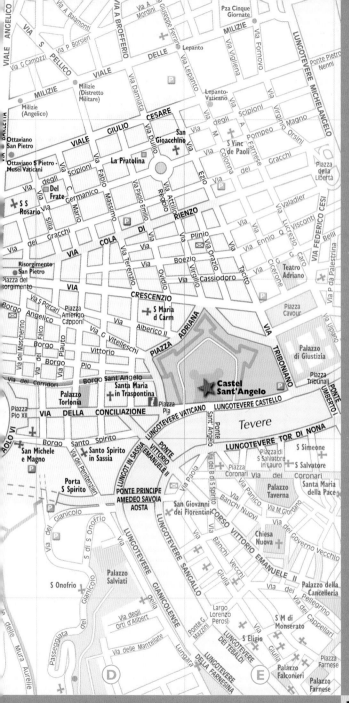

The Vatican and Around
Quick Reference Guide

Basilica di San Pietro (▷ 14)

St. Peter's Basilica was built over the site where the Apostle St. Peter was supposedly buried in the first century. The current church, created over a century, replaced an older church founded around AD326. Piazza San Pietro provides a grand setting for the church, whose vast interior contains a wealth of art and decoration, including Michelangelo's sculptural masterpiece, the *Pietà*.

Castel Sant'Angelo (▷ 16)

The circular bastion of the Castel Sant'Angelo has dominated the banks of the River Tiber since AD130, when the Emperor Hadrian built it as a mausoleum for himself and his imperial successors. In time it became a papal fortress, connected to the Vatican by a covered passageway, and later a prison and a barracks. Today, it is a museum, offering a wide range of papal, military and other exhibits.

Musei Vaticani e Cappella Sistina (▷ 26)

The world's largest museum complex contains many of the artistic treasures accumulated by the papacy in the course of almost 2,000 years. The Sistine Chapel, which lies within the complex, is covered in frescoes by some of the greatest painters of their day, and overarched by Michelangelo's great ceiling fresco and his painting of the *Last Judgment*.

Angel with the Crown of Thorns on Ponte Sant'Angelo

CITY TOURS

Farther Afield

Rome's periphery contains several historical sights, notably a fine bath complex and a cluster of catacombs on the Via Appia Antica. To the east, Tivoli, home to three villas, is one of Rome's most popular excursions. Both of these itineraries can be done as day trips.

DAY 1 Morning
A long morning can easily be devoted to the sights that are gathered conveniently south and southeast of the city center. Start by taking a bus (75, 118 or Archeobus) or the metro to see the **Circo Massimo** (▷ 66), a large open area that was once a Roman race track, and then the **Terme di Caracalla** (▷ 77), an ancient bath complex.

Mid-morning
Take bus 118, 160 or 628 from the Terme to the cluster of sights concentrated on or near the Via Appia Antica, the well-preserved remains of one of ancient Rome's earliest roads. Here you can see the **catacombs of San Callisto and Sebastiano** (▷ 76), along with the roadside tombs of eminent ancient Romans such as Geta and Cecilia Metella. Not far away are three more catacombs, the **Catacombe Ebraiche** (Jewish Catacombs), **Catacombe di San Domitilla** and **Catacombe di Prestato**.

Lunch
It makes sense to pack a lunch to eat on the **Via Appia Antica**. Alternatively, the area near the start of the Via Appia Antica, around the church of the **Domine Quo Vadis**, has cafés and one or two restaurants, notably **Priscilla** (▷ 150).

Afternoon
Return by Archeobus to Piazza della Bocca della Verità. Cross the river to Lungotevere dell'Anguillara, where you can pick up bus 125 to the corner of Via Garibaldi and Via di Porta di San Pancrazio for a short uphill walk to **Monte Gianicolo** (▷ 76). On your return, either take the same bus 125 or walk back through Trastevere.

DAY 2 Morning
A visit to **Tivoli** (▷ 79) makes the most of a full day, but avoid Mondays, when some sights are shut, and, if possible, weekends, when the town is especially busy with Roman day-trippers. A train from Termini is the best way to get there—take the earliest you can manage and remember to validate your train tickets by punching them in the platform machines. On arrival, make straight for the town's well-signed main villa and garden, the **Villa d'Este** (▷ 79).

Mid-morning
The **Villa d'Este** could easily occupy you all morning, but if you still have an hour or so before lunch, consider seeing the town's second villa, the **Villa Gregoriana** (▷ 79), on the opposite (eastern) side of Tivoli.

Lunch
Tivoli sees many visitors, and offers numerous, often poor-quality cafés and restaurants. **Ristorante Sibilla** (▷ 150), which dates from 1730, used to be one such, but the quality of the food and service has recently improved, and the views from the terrace garden over the Aniene gorge are as good as ever. It's convenient for the **Villa Gregoriana** (▷ 79), located on a small street just north of the bridge across the Aniene.

Afternoon
After lunch, return to Piazza Garibaldi, Tivoli's main square, where you can pick up a bus (CAT 4 or 4X) to the third of Tivoli's main attractions, the **Villa Adriana** (▷ 79), whose extensive site should easily keep you occupied for the whole afternoon. Return to Tivoli by bus 4 or 4X and then take the train to Termini (or use bus and metro).

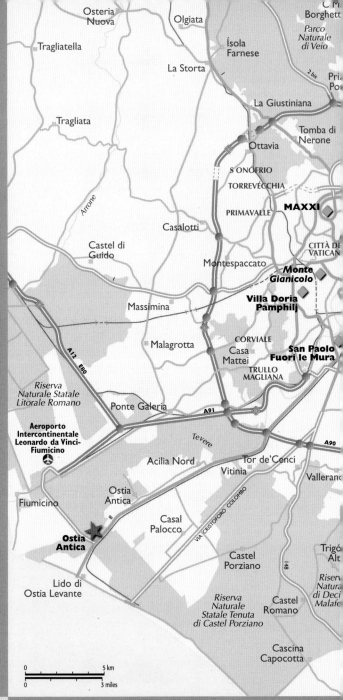

Osteria
Nuova

Olgiata

Borghett

Tragliatella

Ísola
Farnese

Parco
Naturale
di Veio

La Storta

2 bis

Pri
Po

La Giustiniana

Tragliata

Tomba di
Nerone

Ottavia

S ONÓFRIO

TORREVÉCCHIA

Arrone

PRIMAVALLE

MAXXI

Casalotti

CITTÀ DE
VATICAN

Castel di
Guido

Montespaccato

Monte
Gianicolo

Villa Doria
Pamphilj

Massimina

CORVIALE

Malagrotta

Casa
Mattei

San Paolo
Fuori le Mura

TRULLO
MAGLIANA

A12 E80

Riserva
Naturale Statale
Litorale Romano

Ponte Galeria

A91

Tevere

A90

Aeroporto
Intercontinentale
Leonardo da Vinci-
Fiumicino

Acilia Nord

Tor de'Cenci

Vitinia

Vallerand

Fiumicino

Ostia
Antica

Casal
Palocco

VIA CRISTOFORO COLOMBO

Ostia
Antica

Trigó
Alt

Castel
Porziano

I 48

Riser
Natura
di Deci
Malafe

Lido di
Ostia Levante

Riserva
Naturale
Statale Tenuta
di Castel Porziano

Castel
Romano

Cascina
Capocotta

0   5 km
0   3 miles

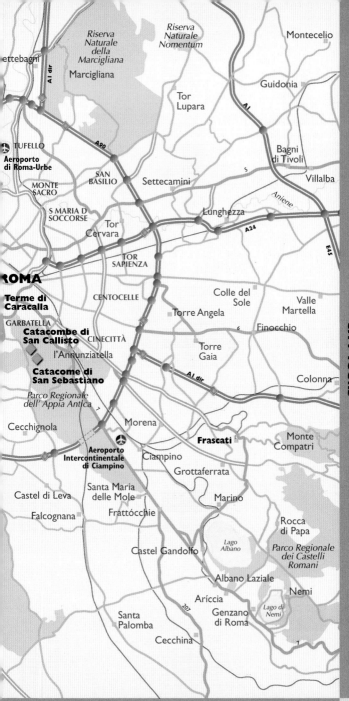

Montecelio

Riserva
Naturale
della
Marcigliana

Riserva
Naturale
Nomentum

Marcigliana

Guidonia

Tor
Lupara

ettebagni

TUFELLO
Aeroporto
di Roma-Urbe

Bagni
di Tivoli

SAN
BASILIO

Settecamini

Villalba

MONTE
SACRO

Aniene

S MARIA D
SOCCORSE

Tor
Cervara

Lunghezza

ROMA

TOR
SAPIENZA

Terme di
Caracalla

CENTOCELLE

Colle del
Sole

Valle
Martella

Torre Angela

GARBATELLA

Catacombe di
San Callisto

CINECITTÀ

Finocchio

l'Annunziatella

Torre
Gaia

Catacome di
San Sebastiano

Colonna

Parco Regionale
dell' Appia Antica

Cecchignola

Morena

Frascati

Monte
Compatri

Aeroporto
Intercontinentale
di Ciampino

Ciampino

Grottaferrata

Castel di Leva

Santa Maria
delle Mole

Marino

Rocca
di Papa

Falcognana

Frattócchie

Lago
Albano

Parco Regionale
dei Castelli
Romani

Castel Gandolfo

Nemi

Albano Laziale

Aríccia

Lago di
Nemi

Santa
Palomba

Genzano
di Roma

Cecchina

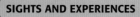

⭐ **TOP 25** SIGHTS AND EXPERIENCES

Ostia Antica (▷ 32–33)
The present Ostia lies not far from Fiumicino airport, southwest of central Rome. Today, it is a small town and modest seaside resort, but 2,000 years ago its ancient Roman counterpart, Ostia Antica—now some way inland—was the main port for the imperial city. The conduit for the immense trade and riches of empire, it rose to prominence in the fourth century BC, and remained Rome's port for around 600 years. As the coast receded it became landlocked and was eventually all but covered in silt and mud. Archaeological excavations have since revealed remarkable remains.

CITY TOURS

MORE TO SEE	64

Catacombe di San Callisto
Catacombe di San Sebastiano
MAXXI
Monte Gianicolo
San Paolo Fuori le Mura
Terme di Caracalla
Villa Doria Pamphilj

ENTERTAINMENT	128

Clubs
Co.So.
Lanficio 159

Sports
Stadio Olimpico

EAT	138

Bars by Day
Bar Necci dal 1924
Roman/Italian
Cacciani

Priscilla
Ristorante Sibilla
Zarazà

Shop

Whether you're looking for the best local products, a department store or a quirky boutique, you'll find them all in Rome. In this section shops are listed alphabetically.

SHOP

Introduction

Rome was once the marketplace of an empire that embraced much of the known world. Today, its shops are tempting enough to provide a serious distraction from the city's cultural delights. You'll find all the great Italian retail staples—food, wine, fashion, shoes, leatherware and clothing—are well represented, and the city is a good source of art, antiques, traditional crafts and artisan products such as furniture.

More for your Money
Mid-price shoes and clothes represent good value for money; you will find them in countless shops around the new city, but particularly Via Nazionale, Via del Tritone and Via del Corso. The same streets are also dotted with small specialist shops selling good-quality bags, gloves and other leatherware. The market near Piazza Vittorio Emanuele II, where many Romans shop, is good for clothes and shoes, as well as pots, pans and kitchenware with an Italian stamp. In stylish Rome, even inexpensive clothes tend to be good quality and well cut.

Designer Names
At the other sartorial extreme, most of the great Italian and other European fashion houses have shops in the city: Gucci, Prada and Armani are all here, in the grid of streets around Via dei

ANTIQUES

It is no wonder, given Rome's long history, that the city is a treasury of antiques. Prices are often high, but the range of objects—Etruscan, Roman, Renaissance, baroque and other items—is unrivaled. For paintings and prints, head for Via Margutta, which also has galleries selling contemporary art and carpets, while for general antiques try Via Giulia, Via del Babuino (Persian carpets), Via dei Coronari, Via dell'Orso and Via del Monserrato. Also good, and with lower prices and less exclusive stock, are Via del Panico, Via del Pellegrino and Via dei Banchi Nuovi.

Clockwise from the top: Window shopping near Piazza San Lorenzo; an attractive arrangement of bottled liqueurs; hats on a stall in Trastevere; shop in style on

Condotti, an excellent source of high-class clothes, shoes, lingerie and accessories. Department stores have not really caught on, and only Coin and Rinascente are worth a visit.

Tempt your Taste Buds

Shopping for food has a unique charm in Rome, whether in the small area shops known as *alimentari*, or the specialist delicatessens in streets such as Via della Croce. The city's markets, particularly Campo de' Fiori, are vibrant sources of provisions. Pasta, the finest extra virgin oil, *funghi porcini* (dried cep mushrooms), truffle oil and spices make good food buys.

Religious Items

The range of shops selling ecclesiastical items is vast. The largest concentration is around St. Peter's—look out for ceramic Swiss Guards and fluorescent rosaries. On Via dei Cestari all manner of ecclesiastic garb is available—if you ever daydreamed about buying a bishop's robe or a cardinal's hat, this is the place.

Fun for the Visitor

Rome has any number of shops and stalls selling plaster and plastic casts of famous statues. Around the tourist traps are plenty of souvenirs, from figures of gladiators to models of the Colosseum. Better-quality items, plus books, prints and artistic replicas, are sold in museum and gallery shops.

MARBLED PAPER

Notebooks and other stationery items covered with marbled paper make wonderful souvenirs, which you can find in shops all over the city. The paper originated in Venice, where the technique arrived from the East in the 15th century, and is still often handmade. The process involves floating multicolor pigments on liquid gum and combing the different colors into distinctive patterns. The paper is placed delicately on top, then lifted and hung up to dry.

Via dei Condotti, a great place for designer clothes and accessories; cooked meats at a deli on Via Marmorata; religious statues for sale near St. Peter's Basilica

Directory

The Ancient City

Department Stores
Coin
Food and Wine
Bottega del Cioccolato
Panella

Central Rome

Accessories and Leather Goods
Mondello Ottica
Beauty
L'Olfattorio
Books and Stationery
Cartoleria Pantheon
Poggi
Fashion
Fabindia
SBU
Food and Wine
Ai Monasteri
Footwear
Borini
Interiors
Bartolucci
Bassetti
De Sanctis

Trastevere and the South

Books and Stationery
Almost Corner Bookshop
Fashion
La Cravatta su Misura
Food and Wine
Drogheria Innocenzi

Northern Rome

Accessories and Leather Goods
Gucci
Books and Stationery
Pineider
Department Stores
La Rinascente
Footwear
Ferragamo
Interiors
Bottega di Marmoraro
C.U.C.I.N.A.
Men's Fashion
Ermenegildo Zegna
Women's Fashion
Marella

Vatican and Around

Food and Wine
Castroni
Franchi (Benedetto Franchi)

Shopping A–Z

AI MONASTERI
aimonasteri.it
This unusual, rather dark old shop sells the products of seven Italian monasteries, from cosmetics, honeys, wines, natural preserves and liqueurs to herbal cures and elixirs offering everything from everlasting love to eternal youth.
➕ F5 ✉ Piazza Cinque Lune 76 (corner of Corso del Rinascimento) ☎ 06 6880 2783 🕐 Mon–Sat 10.30–7.30; closed part of Aug

ALMOST CORNER BOOKSHOP
This tiny bookshop stocks an interesting and unusual selection of English-language books. The prices are competitive, and it is particularly good on biography and history, with a strong emphasis on Rome and Italy. Staff are both helpful and knowledgeable.
➕ E7 ✉ Via del Moro 45 ☎ 06 583 6942 🕐 Mon–Sat 10–1.30, 3.30–8, Sun 11–1.30, 3.30–8; closed Sun in Aug

BARTOLUCCI
bartolucci.com
Bartolucci are renowned wood carvers, with shops in different parts of Italy. Everything in store is hand carved, and it's hard to resist the cheery clocks, toys and kitchen bits and bobs. They specialize in Pinnochios, which come in every size imaginable—there's one riding a bicycle that welcomes shoppers to the store.
➕ G5 ✉ Via dei Pastini 98 ☎ 06 6919 0894 🕐 Daily 10–10

BASSETTI
fratellibassetti.com
Italy has a long tradition of dressmaking and bespoke tailoring, and many Romans have their clothes custom made. Bassetti is where they buy the fabrics, and there's a bewildering range of every conceivable textile at this enticing store. You'll find bolts of silk, wool, jersey, linen, cotton and brocade, as well as wonderful accessories and household linens of all descriptions.
➕ E5 ✉ Corso Vittorio Emanuele II 73 ☎ 06 689 2325 🕐 Tue–Fri 9.30–7.30, Sat 10–7, Mon 3.30–7.30

BORINI
Shoes are piled everywhere in this gloriously crammed shop, with something on offer in myriad colors for every occasion and every taste. Expect value for money and shoes that will last.
➕ F5 ✉ Via dei Pettinari 86 ☎ 06 687 5670 🕐 Tue–Sat 10–7.30, Mon 11–7.30

BOTTEGA DEL CIOCCOLATO
labottegadelcioccolato.it
Most goodies in this chocolate shop are produced from a 19th-century Piedmontese recipe; others are "secrets of old masters."

Window-shopping

There are period cupboards and shelves, and a mirror reflects the chocolate creations in jars along the wall. A second outlet has opened at Via del Vantaggio 22a.

➕ J6 ✉ Via Leonina 82 ☎ 06 482 1473 🕐 Mon–Sat 9.30–7.30; closed mid-Jun to Sep

BOTTEGA DI MARMORARO

It's nice to know that marble, beloved of the Roman emperors, is still worked today in Rome. This tiny hole-in-the-wall shop cum workshop is dedicated to restoring and sourcing antique marble, but also pulls in visitors searching for an original souvenir—a marble plaque or tablet engraved with any inscription you like in Latin, Italian or the Roman dialect.

➕ G3 ✉ Via Margutta 53b ☎ 06 320 7660 🕐 Mon–Sat 8–7.30

CARTOLERIA PANTHEON

pantheon-roma.com

Founded in 1910, this stationery shop sells hand-crafted writing materials of every type. Notebooks, albums and address books are bound in soft leather or marbled paper, and they also offer a vast variety of writing accessories and bags. If you've always wanted a quill pen or a customized seal for wax, this is the place to come.

➕ F5 ✉ Via della Rotonda 15 ☎ 06 687 5313 🕐 Mon–Fri 10.30–8, Sun 1–8

CASTRONI

castroni.com

Castroni boasts Rome's largest selection of imported delicacies, a mouthwatering array of Italian specialties, the finest wines and oils and an amazing range of coffees. It has 12 outlets around the city.

➕ D3 ✉ Via Cola di Rienzo 196–198, corner of Via Terenzio ☎ 06 687 4383 🕐 Mon–Sat 8–8

COIN

coin.it

One of Rome's most popular department stores, Coin is a modern, mainly glass building with cosmetics, home furnishings, kitchenware, toys and fashions. The top floor is dedicated to home exhibitions. Prices are generally higher than in the average store.

➕ M8 ✉ Piazzale Appio 7 ☎ 06 708 0020 🕐 Mon–Sat 10–8, Sun 10.30–8

LA CRAVATTA SU MISURA

cravattasumisura.it

Italian style is to the fore at this store, with multi-hued ties in finest Italian silk and British wool draped elegantly across the fittings. The USP is that they can make you a beautiful piece of neckwear to your own specifications in a day or so—or, if pushed, in a few hours.

➕ F8 ✉ Via di Santa Cecilia 12 ☎ 06 8901 6941 🕐 Mon–Sat 10–7

GIFTS WITH A TWIST

For a souvenir with a difference, visit the extraordinary shops on Via dei Cestari, just south of the Pantheon, which specialize in all sorts of religious clothes, candles and vestments. Crucifixes, rosaries, statues of saints and other religious souvenirs can be found in shops on Via di Porta Angelica near the Vatican. Alternatively, visit the Farmacia Santa Maria della Scala (✉ Piazza Santa Maria della Scala 23 ☎ 06 580 6217 🕐 Mon–Sat 8.30–8.30, Sun 10.30–8.30), an 18th-century monastic pharmacy that sells a variety of herbal remedies.

SHOP

C.U.C.I.N.A.

cucinastore.com

A series of long, narrow rooms opens up as you enter this temple to kitchen wares and gadgetry. Pots, pans, molds, pasta makers, dishes, bowls and platters are piled high and every spare corner is filled with incredibly tempting kitchen aids you barely realized you needed, from garlic presses to bamboo rice steamers.

🔲 G3 ⊠ Via Mario de' Fiori 65 ☎ 06 679 1275 🕲 Daily 10–7.30

DE SANCTIS

desanctis1890.com

Italy's wonderfully vibrant and colorful ceramics are hand crafted all over the country and this store sells pottery of every type from Tuscany, Umbria, Sicily and elsewhere. You can decorate your home and stock your kitchen and dining room, all at prices that may be surprisingly affordable. They also offer a shipping service for heavier items.

🔲 G5 ⊠ Piazza di Pietra 24 ☎ 06 6880 6810 🕲 Mon–Sat 10–1.30, 3–7.30

DROGHERIA INNOCENZI

Set on bustling Piazza San Cosimato, this foodie's haven is stacked to the ceiling with sacks of pasta and polenta, regional specialties, such as honey and olive oil, and products from abroad that are difficult to find elsewhere. People travel from far and wide to stock up on the vast array of products on offer, aided by the friendly and attentive staff.

🔲 E8 ⊠ Piazza San Cosimato, corner of Via Natale del Grande 31 ☎ 06 581 2725 🕲 Daily 8.30–1.30, 4.30–8; closed Thu pm and part of Aug

ERMENEGILDO ZEGNA

zegna.com

Generally considered to be one of Rome's top menswear stores, the accent here is on quintessential Italian style, where the casual clothes are as elegant as the tailored ones. Come here for informal suits and jackets in exquisite, expensive fabrics, as well as stylish shirts, cashmere sweaters and accessories.

🔲 G4 ⊠ Via dei Condotti 58 ☎ 06 6994 0678 🕲 Mon–Sat 10–7.30, Sun 10–7

FABINDIA

fabindia.it

Facing the Ponte Sant'Angelo is this delightful emporium selling Indian fabrics, scarves and garments, all handwoven and made in Indian villages. The company is devoted to developing fair and equitable relationships with the producers. The styles are both traditional and more contemporary, and textiles range from the finest, lightest silks to heavy embroidered cottons.

🔲 E5 ⊠ Via del Banco di Santo Spirito 40 ☎ 06 6889 1230 🕲 Mon–Sat 10–1.30, 3–7.30, Sun 11–7

SHOP

FERRAGAMO

ferragamo.com

This long-established family fashion house is probably Italy's most renowned shoe shop. They also sell handbags, small leather goods, jewelry, timepieces, men's and women's clothes and accessories. The company has expanded into textiles and fragrances, and its collections feature new designs twice a year.

🔒 G4 ✉ Via Condotti 73–74 (women's) ☎ 06 679 1565

🔒 G4 ✉ Via Condotti 65 (men's) ☎ 06 678 1130 ⏰ Mon–Sat 10–7.30, Sun 11–7

FRANCHI

This is quite simply one of the best delicatessens in town, with everything on offer from salamis, antipasti, cheeses and wines to succulent roast meats, fish, salads and sumptuous delicacies for a picnic.

🔒 D3 ✉ Via Cola di Rienzo 200/204 ☎ 06 687 4651 ⏰ Mon–Sat 9–8.30

ROMAN MARKETS

Rome's daily food markets are a good choice to rustle together a picnic, grab some take-home food gifts or add a few iconic images to the holiday snapshot collection. For sheer picturesque charm, Campo de' Fiori heads the list, but don't miss San Cosimato in Trastevere or the Nuovo Mercato in happening Testaccio. Weekends see a fabulous farmers' market, known as the Mercato Campagna Amica, near the Circo Massimo, selling produce from the countryside around Rome, and Via Porta Pratese pulls in the crowds on Sundays for its famous flea market. For bags, shoes and inexpensive clothes head to the Mercato di Via Sannio, right by San Giovanni in Laterano.

GUCCI

gucci.com

Expensive, quality bags, shoes, accessories and leather goods for men and women by this famous name are for sale.

🔒 G3 ✉ Via Condotti 8 ☎ 06 679 0405 ⏰ Mon–Sat 10–7.30, Sun 11–7

MARELLA

marella.com

Understated, easy elegance is Marella's key look, and you'll find a wide range of their latest designs at this flagship store. Their designs are classic with a twist and offer excellent value for money. There is also an outlet at Via del Corso 89 (tel 06 678 5771).

🔒 G4 ✉ Via Frattina 129–31 ☎ 06 6992 38000 ⏰ Tue–Sat 10–7.30, Mon, Sun 11–2, 3–7

MONDELLO OTTICA

mondelloottica.it

Eyewear with a difference is the selling point here. Prices may be higher than average, but the glasses are superlative in quality and sheer chic. Prescription glasses can be made within a day.

🔒 E5 ✉ Via del Pellegrino 98 ☎ 06 686 1955 ⏰ Tue–Sat 10–1.30, 4–7.30

L'OLFATTORIO

olfattorio.it

This delightful store stocks essences from names such as Diptyque, Artisan Parfumeur and Coudray, which the knowledgeable staff will blend, with your help, into a bespoke fragrance just for you—a memorable experience for which it's wise to book ahead.

🔒 G5 ✉ Via di Ripetta 34 ☎ 06 361 2325 ⏰ Thu–Tue 10.30–7.30, Wed 10–7.30

Roman supermarkets are few and far between and most food is still bought in tiny local shops known as *alimentari*. Every street of every "village" or district in the city has one or more of these general shops, a source of everything from olive oil and pasta to candles and corn and bunion treatments. They are also good places to buy picnic provisions—many sell bread and wine—and most have a delicatessen counter that will make you a sandwich (*panino*) from the meats and cheeses on display. For something a little more special, or for food gifts to take home, visit Via della Croce, a street renowned for its wonderful delicatessens.

PANELLA

panellaroma.com

For more than a century, Panella, located in the heart of Rome, has sold dozens of varieties of bread and cakes, and it has the largest selection of homemade *grissini* (bread sticks) in Rome. The back rooms are packed with hard-to-find ingredients. Panella is also an outstanding bar and café, with pleasant tables on the terrace outside (heated in winter).

➕ K6 ✉ Via Merulana 54–55 ☎ 06 487 2435 🕐 Mon–Thu 8am–11pm, Fri–Sat 8am–midnight, Sun 8.30–4

PINEIDER

pineider.com

Pineider, Rome's most exclusive stationer, ships worldwide, so if you buy here you can re-order on-line. They sell beautiful high-quality leather office bags and cases, wallets, fine pens and pencils, but are most noted for their huge range of stationery—writing paper, note-cards, notebooks and bookmarks are all on offer, sold either as boxed sets or individually. They will print personalized headings and have a wide choice of visiting card designs. There's a second outlet at Via dei Due Macelli 68 (tel 06 678 9013, daily 10–7).

➕ H4 ✉ Via della Fontanella Borghese 22 ☎ 06 687 8369 🕐 Daily 10–2, 3–7

POGGI

poggi1825.it

Vivid pigments, lovely papers and canvases and exquisitely soft brushes have been on sale at Poggi's since 1825. The second shop in Trastevere sells a range of high-quality paper.

➕ G5 ✉ Via del Gesù 74–75 ☎ 06 679 3674 🕐 Mon–Sat 9–2, 3–7.30
➕ F8 ✉ Via Cardinal Merry del Val 18/19 ☎ 06 581 2531 🕐 Mon–Sat 10–7.30

LA RINASCENTE

rinascente.it

This chic department store is good for accessories, cosmetics, homewares and designer and mid-range fashion.

➕ K2 ✉ Piazza Fiume ☎ 06 884 1231 🕐 Mon–Sat 9.30–9.30, Sun 10–9

SBU

sbu.it

If you're tracking down cutting-edge Roman super-cool, head to this converted 19th-century work-shop, the headquarters of Strategic Business Unit, famed for their superbly cut jeans. These are mainly made in Italy from finest Japanese denim, but there are Japanese pieces too, plus shirts, sweaters, jackets and women's wear and interesting jewelry.

➕ F5 ✉ Via di San Pantaleo 68–69 ☎ 06 6880 2547 🕐 Mon–Sat 10–7.30

Entertainment

Once you've done with sightseeing for the day, you'll find lots of other great things to do with your time in this chapter, even if all you want to do is relax with a drink. In this section establishments are listed alphabetically.

Introduction

In such a striking city, and one whose climate is so benign, a stroll on a balmy evening might be all the entertainment you need. At the same time, Rome offers world-class classical concerts, recitals in churches, and plenty of jazz, blues and other live music. Films and productions in Italian mean cinema and theater are less accessible to most visitors, but opera and sport—notably football and rugby's Six Nations—transcend language. So, too, do the pleasures of a late-night drink or dance in one of the city's many bars and clubs.

Locations

City-center nightlife focuses on the streets around Piazza Navona (▷ 46–47), and the Campo de' Fiori, home to numerous bars, clubs and restaurants. They're still buzzing, but with an increasingly foreign and often younger, rowdier crowd, and some areas are, at times, pretty insalubrious. This also applies to Trastevere, popular with visitors, late at night.

Nowadays, Romans head to other neighbor-hoods, notably Testaccio, Ostiense and Pigneto. The first two lie south of the city center (get there by bus or taxi) and have excellent restaurants and great clubs—there's a cluster around Monte Testaccio. The Pigneto district, east of the Lateran and noted for its cutting-edge

SUMMER IN THE CITY

Rome's warm summer evenings are conducive to eating and drinking under the stars or strolling to Piazza San Pietro, the Trevi Fountain, Spanish Steps or Colosseum to people-watch and admire the floodlit monuments. The old Ghetto area is charming after dark, and the Pincio, beyond the Spanish Steps, is a great place to watch the sunset. Festivals take place in the city year-round (visit 060608.it), but early June to the end of September sees one of the biggest, the Estate Romana (estateromana. comune.roma.it), with many free events.

BELLA ROM

Clockwise from the top: Taking an evening stroll around Piazza della Rotonda; St. Peter's at dusk; top-quality performers can be heard at classical music events;

street art, is more alternative, with good eating and clubs; you can reach here by tram from Termini to Via Prenestina.

The Musical World

The Auditorium Parco della Musica (▷ 133), Rome's much-loved main performance space, is rightly celebrated for its eclectic program of classical and other music. The city also has a plethora of small musical associations such as the Associazione La Stravaganza (▷ 133) that organize chamber music and other concerts, often in historic settings. Opera in the city, while not as elevated as in Milan or Naples, also benefits from striking settings, notably the Teatro dell'Opera di Roma (▷ 137) and the outdoor Terme di Caracalla (▷ 77). Churches host musical events, not least Sant'Anselmo on the Aventino (▷ 66), where the monks often chant Gregorian plainsong nightly at 7.15.

The Night is Free

Plenty of Rome's nightlife and entertainment costs nothing. Church recitals are often free, and some clubs charge nothing, or next to nothing, during the week. Taking an *aperitivo* is increasingly popular, and many bars offer extensive free snacks with an early-evening drink. Festivals throughout the year often have free events, especially those organized by the city council, the Comune di Roma.

NEED TO KNOW

Entry to clubs during the week is usually free, but at weekends you'll pay an entrance fee and may have to buy a *tessera* (temporary membership). Note that many dance clubs close for the summer, or move to outdoor venues on the coast at, or near, Ostia. For information on nightlife and cultural events, ask hotel concierges, look for fliers, consult *Trovaroma* (a listings magazine free with Thursday's *La Repubblica* newspaper), pick up *Roma Cè* (in shops and bars) or go online at 060608.it.

enjoy a night of live jazz at a club; there are plenty of bars and clubs to choose from in the city center; early-evening cocktails are a popular start to the night

Directory

The Ancient City

Bars and Clubs
Oppio Caffè
Pubs and Bars
Druid's Den

Central Rome

Bars and Clubs
Cabala
Etabli
Salotto 42
Concerts
Associazione la Stravaganza
Wine Bars
Cul de Sac
Escopazzo

Trastevere and the South

Bars and Clubs
Akab-Cave
L'Alibi
Bar San Calisto
Big Mama
Caffè Latino
Freni e Frizioni

Ombre Rosse
Ripa Place
Cinemas and Theaters
Nuovo Sacher
Teatro Vascello
Wine Bars
Enoteca Trastevere

Northern Rome

Bars and Clubs
Stravinskij Bar
Concert Halls and Theaters
Auditorium Parco della Musica
Silvano Toti Globe Theatre
Teatro Olimpico
Opera
Teatro dell'Opera di Roma

Farther Afield

Bars and Clubs
Alexanderplatz
Co.So.
Lanificio 159
Sports
Stadio Olimpico

Entertainment A–Z

AKAB-CAVE
akabclub.com
In the lively Testaccio area, this popular and long-established club is on two levels with a garden area and varied music. Live rock bands and international DJs preside.
➕ Off map at G9 ✉ Via di Monte Testaccio 68–69 ☎ 06 5725 0585 🕐 Thu–Sat 11pm–4.30am 🚇 Piramide 🚌 83, 170, 781 to Piazza di Porta San Paolo or Via Monte Testaccio 💶 Expensive

ALEXANDERPLATZ
alexanderplatzjazzclub.it
Historic jazz club with live bands.
➕ C3 ✉ Via Ostia 9 ☎ Information 06 8377 5604 (after 6pm) 🕐 Sep–Jun daily 8pm–1am 🚇 Ottaviano 🚌 19, 32, 49, 70, 180, 490, 590, 913, 982 to Largo Trionfale-Viale delle Milizie 💶 4-month membership (expensive); usually free to tourists (passport required)

L'ALIBI
Primarily a gay club, but not exclusively, L'Alibi is one of the most reliable (and most established) clubs that have mushroomed in the popular area of Testaccio.
➕ Off map at G9 ✉ Via Monte Testaccio 40–44 ☎ 06 574 3448 🕐 Fri–Sat

midnight–4am 🚇 Piramide 🚌 83, 170, 781 to Piazza di Porta San Paolo or Via Monte Testaccio 💷 Expensive

ASSOCIAZIONE LA STRAVAGANZA

lastravaganza.it

This musical association hosts recitals in historic venues, including the Palazzo Doria Pamphilj, the Chiostro del Bramante in Santa Maria della Pace (near Piazza Navona), Palazzo della Cancelleria (off Campo de' Fiori) and others.

❓ Tickets online at argentia.com

AUDITORIUM PARCO DELLA MUSICA

auditorium.com

This splendid addition to Rome's classical and contemporary music scene has three concert halls in the shape of enormous gray pods set around a vast open-air arena.

➕ Off map at F1 ✉ Viale Pietro de Coubertin 30 ☎ Infoline 06 8024 1281. Ticket office 829101 (from Italy only, toll line) 🚇 Flaminio then tram 2 🚌 53, 168, 910, 982 💷 Moderate

BAR SAN CALISTO

Bohemian and vibrant San Calisto is where the locals tend to hang out. The piazza-side tables give a window on the real Trastevere and cheap prices make it a great spot to linger. Chocolate, hot with cream in winter and cooling as a *gelato* in summer, is among Rome's best.

➕ E7 ✉ Piazza di San Calisto 3 ☎ 06 583 5869 🕐 Mon–Sat 6am–2am 🚌 H, 8 to Viale di Trastevere

BIG MAMA

bigmama.it

Big Mama's been around a long time, and still draws the crowds to its low-ceilinged basement space in Trastevere. Locals consider it Rome's best blues club, so come here for mellow sounds or pick a night when the accent's on jazz, soul or R and B. It's a very popular place so call in advance if you want to book a table.

➕ F8 ✉ Vicolo San Francesco a Ripa 18 ☎ 06 581 2551 🕐 Mid-Sep to Jun Tue–Sat 9pm–1.30am 🚌 H, 8 to Viale di Trastevere 💷 Membership (moderate)

CABALA

Located just north of Piazza Navona, Cabala occupies three floors of an historic medieval building, with a piano bar, restaurant and club, plus a terrace with a glorious view over the Tiber. It is

One of Rome's lively clubs

intimate and exclusive, so be sure to dress up. Booking a table is recommended. The minimum age for entry is 25.

🚼 F4 ⊠ Via dei Soldati 25, near corner of Via dell'Orso ☎ 06 6830 1192, 06 9887 5845 or 329 037 0784 🕐 Fri–Sat 11.30pm–4am 🚌 C3, 70, 81, 87 to Via Zanardelli

CAFFÈ LATINO

caffèlatinoroma.it

Testaccio's oldest club is devoted to eating, drinking, live music and dance sessions—mostly jazz, but also rap, blues and other genres.

🚼 Off map at G9 ⊠ Via Monte Testaccio 96 ☎ 06 578 2411 🕐 Sep–Jul Thu–Sat 10.30pm–4am 🚇 Piramide 🚌 3, 23, 30, 75, 130, 280, 716 to Via Marmorata 💵 Membership (expensive)

CO.SO.

This tiny, stylish, state-of-the-art bar, with its glass shelves of back-lit bottles, is a perfect example of what Pigneto nightlife is all about—laid-back, sharply elegant, cutting edge. It buzzes nightly with people, who come to sample the eclectic cocktails and mixed drinks.

🚼 Off map at M8 ⊠ Via Braccia da Montone 80 ☎ 06 4543 5428 🕐 Mon–Sat 7pm–3am 🚌 81, 150, 412, 810, tram 5, 14, 19

CUL DE SAC

enotecaculdesacroma.it

Rome's original informal wine bar, near Piazza Navona, has pine tables and a big marble bar. More than 1,400 wines are on offer, plus snacks, light meals and cheese and salami from every region in Italy.

🚼 F5 ⊠ Piazza Pasquino 73 ☎ 06 6880 1094 🕐 Daily 12–12 🚌 46, 62, 64 to Corso Vittorio Emanuele II

DRUID'S DEN

druidspubrome.com

This friendly Irish pub appeals to Romans and expats alike. Also try the Fiddler's Elbow, a popular sister pub around the corner at Via dell'Olmata 43 (tel 06 487 2110, daily 4pm–1.30am).

🚼 K6 ⊠ Via San Martino ai Monti 28 ☎ 06 4890 4781 🕐 Daily 5pm–2am 🚇 Cavour 🚌 75, 117 to Via Cavour or 16, 70, 71, 360 to Piazza Santa Maria Maggiore

ENOTECA TRASTEVERE

enotecatrastevere.it

Shelves groaning with bottles line the brick walls of this very popular inviting wine bar in the heart of Trastevere, whose tables spill outside during the summer. You will find more than 900 wines to choose from, predominantly Italian, and they offer a weekly selection of both reds and whites available by the glass or bottle. You can eat a light meal too, and weekends bring live piano music.

🚼 F7 ⊠ Via della Lungaretta 86 ☎ 06 588 5659 🕐 Daily noon–2am 🚌 H, 8, 780 to Piazza Sidney Sonnino

ESCOPAZZO

escopazzo.it

This intimate bar, with its warm wood and sleek steel decor, lies just off Piazza Venezia and offers DJ sets several nights a week. There's occasional live music, while Thursday evenings draw the crowds for karaoke night. It's also popular for private parties, so check ahead for what's happening on the evening you choose to visit.

🚼 G6 ⊠ Via d'Aracoeli 41 ☎ 06 678 4371 🕐 Daily 10am–3am 🚌 40, 64, 170 and other services to Piazza Venezia

ETABLI
etabli.it

Open all hours, Etabli is a real find, a welcoming, relaxed bar-lounge-restaurant that's housed in a 16th-century palazzo just west of Piazza Navona. Sit at a scrubbed wooden table or sink into a leather armchair for breakfast, brunch, tea or dinner—or simply pop in for a drink. The menu offers well-sourced cheeses and *salumi*, there's home baking and a great range of fresh juices and smoothies, as well as every imaginable type of alcohol.

➕ E5 ✉ Vicolo delle Vacche 9a ☎ 06 9761 6694 🕐 Mon–Sat 7am–1.30am, Sun 9am–1am 🚌 46, 62, 64 to Corso Vittorio Emanuele II

FRENI E FRIZIONI
freniefrizioni.com

At the heart of Trastevere, this sleek, modern bar offers the chance to drink and eat light meals either in the pared-down interior or outside in the small piazza.

➕ E7 ✉ Via del Politeama 4–6 ☎ 06 4549 7499 🕐 Daily 6.30pm–2am 🚌 H, 8 to Viale di Trastevere

LANIFICIO 159
lanificio159.com

This ex-industrial complex in Rome's northeastern suburbs, once a wool factory, is now home to a multi-purpose venue. It hosts exhibitions, art and photography shows, Sunday markets and

A great spot for an evening drink

workshops, while its underground club space is given over to live gigs and DJ sets by top Roman and international crews.

➕ Off map at M1 ✉ Via Pietralata 159a ☎ 06 4178 0081 🕐 Restaurant daily 12.30–3, 7.30–10.30; exhibition space varies; club usually Thu–Sat 11pm–4am 🚇 Pietralata

NUOVO SACHER
sacherfilm.eu

Although dedicated to Italian film talent, this cinema occasionally shows foreign films in *versione originale* on Monday. It seats up to 360 people; in summer there are screenings in the courtyard.

➕ F8 ✉ Largo Ascianghi 1 ☎ 06 581 8116 🕐 Daily 4–10 🚌 H, 8 to Viale di Trastevere 💶 Moderate

OMBRE ROSSE
ombrerosseintrastevere.it

This is a friendly, intimate all-day and late-night bar in the heart of Trastevere, with walls covered in

MUSIC OUTDOORS

Alfresco recitals often take place throughout the city in summer. Locations include the cloisters of Santa Maria della Pace; the Villa Doria Pamphilj; in the grounds of the Villa Giulia; and the Area Archeologica del Teatro di Marcello from July to September (as part of the Estate al Tempietto, also known as the Concerti del Tempietto, tempietto.it). Venues are subject to change.

ENTERTAINMENT

Enjoy an evening of classical music

music and movie posters, seating outdoors and live music most nights. There's a limited menu of soups, pastas and light meals.
➕ E7 ✉ Piazza Sant'Egidio 12–13 ☎ 06 588 4155 🕐 Daily 10am–2am 🚌 H, 8, 780 to Viale di Trastevere

OPPIO CAFFÈ
oppiocaffe.it
Old, vaulted brick walls are offset by contemporary fittings in this airy café-bar-club on the street immediately north of the Colosseum, by the Colle Oppio park. There are wonderful floodlit views of the amphitheater plus live music some nights, and DJs most Fridays and Saturdays.
➕ J7 ✉ Via delle Terme di Tito 72 ☎ 06 474 5262 🕐 Daily 7am–2am; closed in Aug 🚇 Colosseo 🚌 C3, 3, 51, 85, 87, 117 to Piazza del Colosseo

RIPA PLACE
worldhotelriparoma.com
This stylish café and lounge is part of the four-star Worldhotel Ripa Roma, located in a quiet spot near the Tiber between Via Portuense and Viale di Trastevere. It makes a great place for an early cocktail or aperitif.
➕ E9 ✉ Via degli Orti di Trastevere 1 ☎ 06 58611 🕐 Bar-café 10.30am–11.30pm, restaurant 12.30–2.30, 7.30–11 🚌 H, 8 to Viale di Trastevere

SALOTTO 42
salotto42.space
Sleek design and great comfort give this stylish all-day haunt on lovely Piazza di Pietro something special. You can relax, drink and graze during the day and enjoy cocktails and the superb sound system in the evenings.
➕ G5 ✉ Piazza di Pietro 42 ☎ 06 678 5804 🕐 Tue–Sat 10am–2am, Sun–Mon 10am–midnight 🚌 C3, 51, 62, 63, 80, 117 to Via del Corso

SILVANO TOTI GLOBE THEATRE
globetheatreroma.com
This replica Elizabethan theater is modeled on London's Globe. Unlike London, weather is not normally a problem, and you can take in Shakespeare's work under the stars in both Italian and, sometimes, English.
➕ H2 ✉ Largo Aqua Felix, Villa Borghese ☎ 060608 🚌 C3, 53

APERITIVO TIME
The great Torinese predilection for the pre-dinner *aperitivo* has arrived in Rome. Arrive in many bars after 7pm and you can feast or graze on generous snacks of pasta, cold meats, couscous, cheese and much more all for the price of a glass of wine. Popular *aperitivo* bars are opening all the time. You'll find these bars throughout the historic core, particularly around Piazza Navona, and in Trastevere.

STADIO OLIMPICO

Football teams AS Roma and Lazio are based here. Games are played on alternate Sundays.

🔳 Off map at C1 ✉ Via del Foro Italico ☎ 06 323 7333 (box office) or 06 36851 🚇 Ottaviano, then bus 32 to Piazzale della Farnesina/Stadio Tennis

AS Roma information:

Tickets (non-transferable) available at many outlets around Rome. Photo ID required to enter the stadium. Full list of sellers on asroma.com. Also from Lottomatica stores and AS Roma outlets (✉ Piazza Colonna 360 ☎ 06 6978 1232/ 06 6920 0642)

Lazio information:

Tickets can be bought online at sslazio.it. Also at Lottomatica stores or authorized outlets (details at sslazio.it) ☎ 02 6006 0900

STRAVINSKIJ BAR

roccofortehotels.com

Picasso and the writer Jean Cocteau whiled away hours in these gardens, now the setting for a pretty, if expensive, hotel bar.

🔳 G3 ✉ De Russie Hotel, Via del Babuino 9 ☎ 06 328 881 🕐 Daily 9am–1am 🚇 Flaminio 🚌 117

TEATRO OLIMPICO

teatroolimpico.it

The Filarmonica di Roma performs here, as well as other international dance and music ensembles.

🔳 Off map at F1 ✉ Piazza Gentile da Fabriano 17 ☎ Box Office 06 481 7003 or 06 4816 0255 🚌 910 to Pannini or metro A to Flaminio, then tram 2 to Piazza Mancini

TEATRO DELL'OPERA DI ROMA

operaroma.it

One of Italy's top opera houses is also an official venue for ballet. Summer performances are staged outdoors in the Terme di Caracalla.

🔳 J–K5 ✉ Piazza Beniamino Gigli 1 ☎ 06 481 601/06 488 1755 🚇 Termini 🚌 H, 40, 60, 64, 70, 71, 170 to Via Nazionale or services to Termini

TEATRO VASCELLO

teatrovascello.it

On the edge of Trastevere, this is a small but good venue for experimental dance. It also hosts classical ballet, multimedia events and children's shows.

🔳 D8 ✉ Via Giacinto Carini 78 ☎ 06 589 8031 🕐 Sep–Jun Tue–Sat 5.30–9, Sun 3–5 🚌 44, 75, 710, 870

Wine bar in Trastevere

Eat

There are places to eat across the city to suit all tastes and budgets. In this section establishments are listed alphabetically.

EAT

Introduction

Prepare yourself for rich, sun-drenched tastes. Thousands of restaurants cater to every budget and provide every kind of dining experience. Eating is so much a social way of life that it is quite normal to spend several hours over a meal.

What to Eat

Rome is devoted to Italian food, and not the relatively sophisticated food of Bologna or Milan, but a cuisine that has its roots in simple peasant cooking. Staples from elsewhere in the country are available, not least pizza, but the classic Roman dishes are offal (brains, tripe), salt cod, veal, chickpeas and pigs' trotters. Wines are robust and unpretentious, typically the refreshing and inexpensive whites such as Frascati from the Albani hills south of the city.

Where to Eat

Central Rome's restaurants are concentrated in the streets around Piazza Navona and the Pantheon. Trastevere is also a traditional dining area, along with the more outlying Testaccio, Pigneto and San Lorenzo. Romans demand value for money, resulting in the return of traditional *trattorie* and *osterie*, plus the emergence of informal wine bars *(enoteche)*, salad bars, bars with food and Italian-style diners. The food may often be simple, but culinary standards are higher than they used to be.

CUTTING COSTS

In bars, you will pay less for food and drink if you stand at the bar rather than sitting at waiter-service tables. Most have a selection of rolls *(panini)* and sandwiches *(tramezzini)*. For tap, rather than bottled water, ask for *acqua dal rubinetto, per favore.* Pizza by the slice makes a good lunchtime snack—tiny establishments can be found across the city: look for signs "Pizza al Taglio" or "Pizza al Forno." Many *alimentari* (small food shops) will make up a round Roman roll *(una rosetta)* with cheese or ham.

From the top: Pizza or pasta, whatever your choice; visit a deli for delicious bread for a picnic; start the day with a cappuccino

EAT

Directory

The Ancient City

Coffee/Pastries
Antico Caffè del Brasile
Fine Dining
Antonello Colonna Open
Fish/Seafood
San Teodoro
Gelaterie
Gelato Fantasia
Roman/Italian
L'Asino d'Oro
Il Bocconcino
Pasqualino al Colosseo
Silvio alla Suburra

Central Rome

Coffee/Pastries
Bar del Fico
Caffè Farnese
La Caffettiera
Sant'Eustachio
La Tazza d'Oro
Fine Dining
Il Convivio Troiani
Il Pagliaccio
Gelaterie
Gelateria della Palma
Tre Scalini
Pizza/Pasta
Da Baffetto

Roman/Italian
Antica Birreria Peroni
Armando al Pantheon
Le Cave di Sant'Ignazio
Da Francesco
Ditirambo
Grano
'Gusto
Maccheroni
World Cuisines
L'Eau Vive

Trastevere and the South

Fine Dining
Checchino dal 1887
Glass Hosteria
Gelateria
Alberto Pica
Pizza/Pasta
Dar Poeta
Ivo
Panattoni Ai Marmi
Roman/Italian
L'Arcangelo
Casetta de' Trastevere
Checco er Carettiere
Da Felice
Giggetto
Paris
Piperno
Sora Lella
Vecchia Roma

Northern Rome

Gelateria
Il Gelato di San Crispino
Roman/Italian
Matricianella
Vegetarian
Margutta RistorArte

Vatican and Around

Pizza
Pizzarium Bonci
La Pratolina
Roman/Italian
Borgo Nuovo
Dal Toscano
Del Frate

Farther Afield

Bars by Day
Bar Necci dal 1924
Roman/Italian
Cacciani
Priscilla
Ristorante Sibilla
Zarazà

EAT

EAT

ALBERTO PICA €

Alberto Pica offers around 20 varieties of excellent ice cream; try their specialties such as green apple *(mele verde)* and Sicilian citrus *(agrumi di Sicilia)*.

➕ F6 ✉ Via della Seggiola 12 ☎ 06 686 8405 🕐 Daily 8am–midnight, longer hours in summer; closed 2 weeks in Aug 🚌 8 to Via Arenula and 8, 46, 62, 64, 70, 81, 87, 492 to Largo di Torre Argentina

ANTICA BIRRERIA PERONI €

anticabirreriaperoni.net

Generations of Romans and tourists have packed this beer hall for years, quenching their thirst with draft Peroni or one of the other tap beers on offer. Food is straightforward and hearty, with daily changing pasta and meat dishes and a few salads. You can eat standing at the bar if you're pressed for time.

➕ G5 ✉ Via di San Marcello 19 ☎ 06 679 5310 🕐 Mon–Sat 12–12 🚌 63, 81, 87 and all other buses to Piazza Venezia

ANTICO CAFFÈ DEL BRASILE €

A superb variety of beans and ground coffee is sold from huge sacks or at the bar. John Paul II bought his coffee here before his pontificate—try the "Pope's blend."

➕ J6 ✉ Via dei Serpenti 23 ☎ 06 488 2319 🕐 Mon–Sat 6am–8.30pm, Sun 7am–8pm; closed Sat from 2pm and Sun Jun–Aug 🚌 60, 64, 70, 170 to Via Nazionale or 75, 117 to Via Cavour

ANTONELLO COLONNA OPEN €€–€€€

antonellocolonna.it

Celebrated chef Antonello Colonna has earned Michelin stars for his sophisticated cooking in this futuristic, virtually all-glass restaurant in the Palazzo delle Esposizioni. Go for the good-value City Lunch from Tuesday to Friday (choose from an all-you-can-eat buffet at €16 or brunch at weekends for €30).

➕ H5 ✉ Via Milano 9a, corner of Via Nazionale ☎ 06 4782 2641 🕐 Tue–Sat 12.30–3.30, 7–10.30, Sun 12.30–3.30 🚌 40, 60, 64, 70, 170 and services to Via Nazionale

L'ARCANGELO €€€

larcangelo.com

The wood paneling, old photographs and leather banquettes add to the traditional charm of this restaurant, founded in fact within the last 25 years and one of the first of Rome's eating places to update

THE MENU

Starters are called antipasti; first course (soup, pasta or risotto) is *il primo*; and main meat and fish dishes are *il secondo*. Salads *(insalata)* and vegetables *(contorni)* are ordered (and often eaten) separately. Desserts are *dolci*, with cheese *(formaggio)* or fruit *(frutta)* to follow. If no menu card is offered, ask for *la lista* or *il menù*. A set-price menu *(un menù turistico)* may seem good value, but portions are usually small and the food is invariably poor—usually just spaghetti with a tomato sauce, followed by a piece of chicken and fruit.

the traditional trattoria formula. The food remains excellent, with the menu featuring dishes that display a new twist on old favorites.

✚ E3 ✉ Via Giuseppe Gioacchino Belli 59 ☎ 06 321 0992 🕐 Mon–Fri 1–2.30, 8–11, Sat 8–11 🚇 Lepanto 🚌 30, 49, 70, 87, 130, 990 to Piazza Cavour or Via Cicerone

ARMANDO AL PANTHEON €€
armandoalpantheon.it

Armando's welcoming family has been cooking Roman classics for generations in this wonderfully traditional restaurant in the heart of the *centro storico*, moments from the Pantheon. All the great Roman classic specialties are on the menu, making this one of the best places to enjoy dishes such as *spaghetti alla matriciana* (with spicy ham and tomato), *cacio e pepe* (with sheep's cheese and black pepper) or *saltimbocca alla romana* (veal with sage and ham). Booking is essential.

✚ F5 ✉ Salita dei Crescenzi 31 ☎ 06 6880 3034 🕐 Mon–Fri 12.30–3, 7–11, Sat 12.30–3 🚌 40, 64, 70 and other services to Largo Torre di Argentina

L'ASINO D'ORO €

Not a destination restaurant, but a good-value option on pretty Via del Boschetto, away from the crowds and close to the Forum and Colosseum. The interior is bright, cool and modern, and there are a few tables on the street outside. The food is well presented and more creative than most in Rome: the set €16 lunch menu—different every day—is a bargain.

✚ J6 ✉ Via del Boschetto 73 ☎ 06 4891 3832 🕐 Tue–Sat 12.30–2.30, 7.30–11 🚇 Cavour 🚌 75, 117 to Via Cavour or Via dei Serpenti

Dining in style

BAR DEL FICO €
bardelfico.com

This simple retreat just west of Piazza Navona has been a reliable city-center fixture for decades. Visit for a morning coffee (there are tables inside or out), join Rome's younger crowd at the bar for aperitifs, or try the restaurant for good, straightforward food such as pizza, pasta and gourmet burgers.

✚ E5 ✉ Piazza del Fico 26–28/Via della Pace 34–35 ☎ 06 6889 1373 🕐 Daily 8am–2am 🚌 40, 46, 62, 64 on Corso Vittorio Emanuele II to Chiesa Nuova

BAR NECCI DAL 1924 €–€€
necci1924.com

This all-day bar-restaurant was one of the first of the popular eating and drinking locales that helped put Pigneto on the map. Come here for anything from breakfast to dinner or just for a drink, and enjoy the well-sourced, fresh, seasonal cooking. The easiest access is by taxi or metro, following a visit to San Giovanni in Laterano.

✚ Off map at M8 ✉ Via Fanfulla da Lodi 68 ☎ 06 9760 1552 🕐 Daily 8am–2am 🚇 Pigneto 🚌 16, 51, 81, 85

EAT

Traditional pizzas at Da Baffetto

➕ D4 ✉ Borgo Pio 104 ☎ 06 689 2852
🕐 Daily 12–10; closed Tue Nov–Mar
🚇 Ottaviano 🚌 19, 32, 81, 590 to Piazza
del Risorgimento

CACCIANI €€
cacciani.it
This established hotel restaurant in
the heart of Frascati serves Roman
and classic Italian dishes. Try the
house specialty, *pollo alla romana*
(chicken with a tomato sauce).
✉ Via Armando Diaz 13, Frascati ☎ 06
940 1991 🕐 Tue–Sun 12.30–2.30, 7–10.30;
closed Sun evening Oct–May, and 7–14 Jan,
16–26 Aug

IL BOCCONCINO €
ilbocconcino.com
A recent but traditional-looking
trattoria, Bocconcino offers classic
Roman dishes, though service may
be slow at busy times. It is one of
several good options in the streets
east of the Colosseum—also try
Café Café around the corner at Via
dei SS Quattro 44 for snacks and
light lunches, or Luzzi (closed
Wed), at Via San Giovanni in
Laterano 88, for pizzas.
➕ J7 ✉ Via Ostilia 23 ☎ 06 7707 9175
🕐 Thu–Tue 12.30–3.30, 7.30–11; closed 2
weeks in Aug 🚇 Colosseo 🚌 All services
to the Colosseum

BORGO NUOVO €€
Stop here for freshly prepared
meat, fish, pizza or pasta—or a
salad and sandwich.

CAFFÈ FARNESE €
Quieter and more elegant than the
bars on nearby Campo de' Fiori,
the Farnese serves cakes, ice
creams and light snacks as well as
drinks. There are tables outside on
the cobbled street. Prices in this
part of Rome can be expensive.
➕ E6 ✉ Via dei Baullari 106–107, corner
Piazza Farnese ☎ 06 6880 2125 🕐 Daily
7am–2am 🚌 46, 62, 64 and other services
to Corso Vittorio Emanuele II

LA CAFFETTIERA €
lacaffettieraroma.it
Great coffee and mouth-watering
pastries and cakes are the order of
the day at this bar/tearoom.
➕ G5 ✉ Piazza di Pietro ☎ 06 679 8147
🕐 Mon–Sat 7.30am–9pm, Sun 9–9; closed
Sun Jul–Aug 🚌 C3, 51, 62, 63, 80, 117 to
Via del Corso

UNUSUAL WAITRESSES
You are served at the L'Eau Vive (▷ 147) by nuns from an order known as the Vergini
Laiche Cristiane di Azione Cattolica Missionaria per Mezzo del Lavoro (Christian Virgins of
Catholic Missionary Action through Work). With restaurants in several parts of the world,
their aim is to spread the message of Christianity through the medium of French food. At
9.30pm, during dinner, the nuns sing *Ave Maria*.

CASETTA DE' TRASTEVERE €–€€

This curious restaurant at the heart of Trastevere has tables outside on a quiet square. The appealing interior re-creates a traditional Roman piazza, complete with balconied houses. Expect straightforward Roman cooking.

➕ E7 ✉ Piazza de' Renzi 31a–32 ☎ 06 580 0158 🕐 Daily 12–12 🚌 23, 125, 280 to Ponte Sisto-Piazza Trilussa

LE CAVE DI SANT'IGNAZIO €

dasabatino.it

Also known as Da Sabatino, this restaurant is part of a dying breed of simple, low-cost, family-run central Roman trattorias. Inside there are several dining rooms, usually occupied by locals, plus tables on the pretty and intimate little Piazza Sant'Ignazio outside. The Roman wine and food are unpretentious—pizzas from a wood-fired oven, for example, or cheese and black pepper *cacio e pepe* pasta; the *antipasti* are a meal in themselves.

➕ G5 ✉ Piazza Sant'Ignazio 169, off Via del Seminario ☎ 06 679 7821 🕐 Daily 12.30–3.30, 6.30–midnight 🚌 C3, 51, 62, 63, 80, 83, 85 to Via del Corso

CHECCHINO DAL 1887 €€€

checchino-dal-1887.com

Robust appetites are required for the menu at this Testaccio establishment. Quintessential Roman dishes relying largely on offal are the specialty. There is outdoor seating during the summer. Reservations are advisable.

➕ Off map at G9 ✉ Via Monte Testaccio 30 ☎ 06 574 3816 🕐 Tue–Sat 12.30–3, 8–11; closed Aug, 24 Dec–2 Jan 🚌 3, 75, 118 to Piramide

CHECCO ER CARETTIERE €€–€€€

checcoercarettiere.it

This Trastevere beacon to traditional cooking is adorned with black-and-white celebrity photos. Good seafood and homemade specialties dominate the menu, while a patio and internal garden room cater to smokers.

➕ E7 ✉ Via Benedetta, 10–13 ☎ 06 581 7018 🕐 Daily 12–3, 7.30–midnight 🚌 23, 125, 280 to Piazza Trilussa

IL CONVIVIO TROIANI €€€

ilconviviotroiani.com

The Troiani brothers from the Marche region have created a tranquil little restaurant with a reputation for innovative and subtle modern dishes.

➕ F4 ✉ Vicolo dei Soldati 31 ☎ 06 686 9432 🕐 Mon–Sat dinner only 8–10.30; closed 13–17 Aug 🚌 30, 70, 81, 87, 130, 492 to Corso del Rinascimento

DA BAFFETTO €

pizzeriabaffetto.it

This tiny, hole-in-the-wall pizzeria has retained its atmosphere and low prices. Thin, crisp pizzas fired in a traditional oven are the

---

THE BILL

The bill (check), *il conto*, usually includes extras such as *servizio* (service). Iniquitous cover charges *(pane e coperto)* have now been outlawed, but some restaurants still try to get round the regulations. Only pay for bread *(pane)* if you have asked for it. Proper receipts—not a scrawled piece of paper—must be given by law. If you receive a scrap of paper, which is more likely in a pizzeria, and have doubts about the total, be sure to ask for a proper receipt *(una fattura* or *una ricevuta)*.

specialty. It's very popular so expect to wait for a table, but there is a second outlet, Pizzeria Baffetto 2, near Campo de' Fiori.

🔢 E5 🖂 Via del Governo Vecchio 114 ☎ 06 686 1617 🕚 Daily 6.30pm–1am; closed Aug 🚌 46, 62, 64 to Corso Vittorio Emanuele II

🔢 E5 🖂 Piazza del Teatro di Pompeo 18 ☎ 06 6821 0807 🕚 Wed–Tue 12pm–2am 🚌 40, 46, 62, 64 to Corso Vittorio Emanuele II

DA FELICE €€

feliceatestaccio.com

The Trivelloni family have run this Testaccio restaurant since 1936, serving generations of diners with Roman classic dishes. You can expect artichokes, beans, lentils, spelt, offal, boiled meat and chicken—all seasonal. Specials change daily and this generation of the family have turned the place into one of Rome's most buzzing eating choices. Booking essential.

🔢 Off map at G9 🖂 Via Mastro Giorgio 29, Testaccio ☎ 06 574 6800 🕚 Daily 12.30–3, 8–11.30; closed 3 weeks in Aug 🚇 Piramide 🚌 3, 23, 30, 75, 130, 280 to Via Marmorata

DA FRANCESCO €

dafrancesco.it

This simple restaurant near Piazza Navona has never lost its appeal over the years, thanks to a warm, friendly atmosphere, good Roman food and low prices. There are no reservations, so arrive early or you may have to wait for a table.

🔢 E5 🖂 Piazza del Fico 29 ☎ 06 686 4009 🕚 Daily 12–3.30, 7–12.30 🚌 64 and other services to Chiesa Nuova on Corso Vittorio Emanuele II

DAL TOSCANO €–€€

ristorantedaltoscano.it

This large trattoria north of Piazza San Pietro serves Tuscan food, and is particularly known for its meats and its wood-fired grill.

🔢 C3 🖂 Via Germanico 58/60 ☎ 06 3972 5717 🕚 Tue–Sun 12.30–3, 8–11.15 🚇 Ottaviano 🚌 19, 23, 32, 49, 492 to Piazza del Risorgimento

DAR POETA €

darpoeta.com

A popular pizzeria hidden in a quiet street, Dar Poeta has a simple interior but the pizza and desserts are creative and excellent.

🔢 E7 🖂 Vicolo di Bologna 45 ☎ 06 588 0516 🕚 Daily 12–11 🚌 H, 8, 870 and all services to Trastevere

DEL FRATE €€

enotecadelfrate.it

This attractive, sleek wine bar is just a few minutes' walk from the Vatican Museums. The wine list is superb, with many interesting wines on offer by the glass, and the menu modern, imaginative and lighter than that in many

EAT

Roman eating houses. The cheese list features regional specialties from all over Italy.

🔲 D3 ✉ Via degli Scipioni 118–122 ☎ 06 323 6437 🕙 Mon–Sat 12.30–3, 6.30–1; kitchen closes 11.45 Ⓜ Ottaviano 🚌 23, 49, 492 to Piazza del Risorgimento or 19, 32, 49, 70 to Viale Giulio Cesare

DITIRAMBO €€
ristoranteditirambo.it

The kitchen in this small restaurant uses organic ingredients, and produces homemade bread, pasta and desserts. Expect Italian cooking with a creative twist. Reservations are essential.

🔲 F6 ✉ Piazza della Cancelleria 75 ☎ 06 687 1626 🕙 Tue–Sun 12.45–3.15, 7.30–11.30, Mon 7pm–11.30pm; closed part of Aug 🚌 46, 62, 64 to Corso Vittorio Emanuele II

L'EAU VIVE €€
ristorante-eauvive.it

The menu here is predominantly French, with dishes such as guinea fowl, classic salads and foie gras, and a daily special that's a French take on international cuisine. The dining rooms are elegant, but it's excellent value—there are lunch menus at €10, €14 and €18. You will be served by nuns (▷ panel, 144).

🔲 F5 ✉ Via Monterone 85 ☎ 06 6880 1095 🕙 Mon–Sat 12.30–2.30, 7–10.30; closed Aug 🚌 8, 46, 62, 64, 70, 87, 492 to Largo di Torre Argentina

GELATERIA DELLA PALMA €
dellapalma.it

Choose from more than 100 varieties of ice cream at this big, brash place near the Trevi Fountain. It also offers cakes and chocolates.

🔲 F5 ✉ Via della Maddalena 20 ☎ 06 6880 6752 🕙 Daily 8.30am–midnight or later 🚌 All services to Via del Corso or Corso del Rinascimento

GELATO FANTASIA €

A 10-minute walk from the Forum or the Colosseum will lead you to this fabulous *gelateria*, whose ices are some of the best in Rome. Flavors include eight different types of chocolate, seasonal fruits and salted peanut.

🔲 H9 ✉ Viale Aventino 59 🕙 Mon–Thu 12–10, Fri–Sun 12–11 Ⓜ Circo Massimo 🚌 75, 118, 673

IL GELATO DI SAN CRISPINO €
ilgelatodisancrispino.com

Come here for the delicious ice cream. There's a second outlet at Piazza Maddalena 3 (daily 11am–12.30am, closed Tue Oct–Mar), just north of the Pantheon.

🔲 H4 ✉ Via della Panetteria 42 ☎ 06 679 3924 🕙 Sun–Thu 11am–12.30am, Fri–Sat 11am–1.30am Ⓜ Barberini

GIGGETTO €
giggetto.it

This famous Romano-Jewish restaurant in the Ghetto district has been in business for over 80

BUYING ICE CREAM

Ice cream *(gelato)* in a proper *gelateria* (ice cream shop) is sold either in a cone *(un cono)* or a paper cup *(una coppa)*. Specify which you want and then decide how much you wish to pay. Sizes of cone and cup go up in price bands, usually starting small and ending enormous. You can select up to two or three varieties (more in bigger tubs) and will usually be asked if you want a swirl of cream *(panna)* to round things off.

years. Try the classic *carciofi alla giudea* (Jewish-style artichokes).
➕ G6 ✉ Via Portico d'Ottavia 21a ☎ 06 686 1105 🕐 Tue–Sun 12.30–3, 7.30–11; closed late Jul, Aug 🚌 H, 8, 63 to Via Arenula and 46, 62, 70 and other services to Largo di Torre Argentina

GLASS HOSTERIA €€€
glass-restaurant.it

The contemporary styling of this striking restaurant is a world away from that of the traditional Roman trattoria. The ultra-modern design is matched by excellent, creative Italian cooking that earned a Michelin star in 2011.
➕ E7 ✉ Vicolo delle Cinque 58 ☎ 06 5833 5903 🕐 Tue–Sun 7.30pm–11.30pm 🚌 23, 125, 280 to Ponte Sisto-Piazza Trilussa

GRANO €€
ristorantegrano.it

Whether you love or hate the virtually all-white decor of this faux-rustic bar and restaurant just east of San Luigi dei Francesi, the innovative southern Italian cooking is excellent.

A tempting plate of pasta

➕ F5 ✉ Piazza Rondanini 53 ☎ 06 6819 2096 🕐 Daily 12.30–3, 7.30–12 🚌 30, 70, 81, 87 and other services to Corso del Risorgimento

'GUSTO €€
gusto.it

This chic, modern restaurant spreads over two levels where you can eat pizzas, salads and other light meals downstairs or fuller meals upstairs. There is also a book store and kitchenware shop.
➕ F3 ✉ Piazza Augusto Imperatore 9 ☎ 06 322 6273 🕐 Daily 12.30pm–12.30am 🚌 117 to Via del Corso

IVO €

Lines are common at Trastevere's best-known pizzeria but turnover is quick.
➕ E7 ✉ Via di San Francesco a Ripa 158 ☎ 06 581 7082 🕐 Mon, Wed–Sat 6pm–12.30am, Sun 12–4, 6–12.30; closed 3 weeks Aug 🚌 H, 8, 780 to Viale di Trastevere

MACCHERONI €€
risorantemaccheroni.com

This popular, informal restaurant has several attractive, rustic dining rooms (plus tables outside on the square), though avoid the basement rooms. Attentive staff serve good, traditional Italian dishes.
➕ F5 ✉ Piazza delle Coppelle 44 ☎ 06 6830 7895 🕐 Daily 12.30–3, 7–11.30 🚌 8, 64, 87 and other services to Largo di Torre Argentina and Via del Corso

MARGUTTA RISTORARTE €–€€
ilmargutta.bio

There are few vegetarian restaurants as such; Margutta is the exception, and good value too. Lunch is served buffet style, with over 50 dishes featuring fresh organic vegetables, as well as pasta and pizza. Expect to pay more in the evenings, when you may find live jazz on offer.

🟦 G3 ✉ Via Margutta 118 ☎ 06 3265 0577 🕒 Daily 12.30–11.30 🚇 Spagna 🚌 117

MATRICIANELLA € €

matricianella.it

This trattoria is close to Via del Corso, not far from the parliament building. It offers Roman cooking with the odd twist and has a few outside tables in summer.

🟦 G4 ✉ Via del Leone 4 ☎ 06 683 2100 🕒 Mon–Sat 12.30–3, 7.30–11; closed Sun and 3 weeks in Aug 🚌 All services to Via del Corso

IL PAGLIACCIO €€€

ristoranteilpagliaccio.it

Inventive chef, Anthony Genovese, has won Michelin stars in the past, and this formal gourmet experience continues to be a superb combination of Oriental, Mediterranean and traditional Italian cuisine.

🟦 E5 ✉ Via dei Banchi Vecchi 129 ☎ 06 6880 9595 🕒 Wed–Sat 12.30–2, 7.30–10.30; Tue dinner only; closed Sun, Mon, part Jan, Aug 🚌 40, 46, 62, 64 to Chiesa Nuova on Corso Vittorio Emanuele II

PANATTONI AI MARMI €

Panattoni is known locally as "L'Obitorio" (The Morgue) on account of its characteristic cold marble-topped tables. Watch the flamboyant chef flip the pizzas at the oven. Arrive early to secure a table outside.

🟦 F8 ✉ Viale di Trastevere 53 ☎ 06 580 0919 🕒 Thu–Tue 6.30pm–2am; closed 3 weeks in Aug 🚌 H, 8, 780 to Viale di Trastevere

ROMAN SPECIALTIES

Roman preferences—though they are by no means confined to the city—include pastas such as *bucatini all'amatriciana* (tomato sauce, salt pork and chili peppers); *spaghetti alla carbonara* (egg, bacon, pepper and cheese); and *gnocchi alla Romana* (small potato or semolina dumplings with tomato or butter). The best-known main course is *saltimbocca alla Romana* (veal scallops with ham and sage, cooked in wine and butter). Also traditional are *trippa* (tripe), *cervelli* (brains) and *coda alla vaccinara* (oxtail).

PARIS €€

ristoranteparis.it

This popular little restaurant is particularly known for its fish, pasta dishes and hearty Roman cuisine. There are outside tables. Reserve ahead.

🟦 E7 ✉ Piazza di San Calisto 7a ☎ 06 581 5378 🕒 Tue–Sun 12.30–7.30, 8–11; closed Jan and 3 weeks in Aug 🚌 H, 8 to Piazza Sidney Sonnino or 23, 125, 280 to Lungotevere Sanzio

PASQUALINO AL COLOSSEO €€

This simple, long-established trattoria serves good, robust food near the Colosseum.

🟦 K7 ✉ Via SS. Quattro Coronati 66 ☎ 06 700 4576 🕒 Daily 12–3, 7–11; closed 2 weeks in Aug 🚇 Colosseo 🚌 85, 117 to Via di San Giovanni in Laterano or services to Piazza del Colosseo

PIPERNO €€

ristorantepiperno.com

Much Roman cuisine is based on the city's Jewish culinary traditions. The traditional Piperno has been a temple to Romano-Jewish cuisine for over a century. Try the deep-fried artichokes. This is a very popular destination, especially for Sunday lunch, so reserve ahead.

🔲 F6 ✉ Via Monte de' Cenci 9 ☎ 06 6880 6629/6833 606 🕐 Tue–Sat 12.45–2.30, 7.45–10.30, Sun 12.45–3; closed Aug 🚌 H, 8, 63 to Via Arenula and 8, 46, 62, 64, 70, 87, 492 to Largo di Torre Argentina

PIZZARIUM BONCI €

You can't sit down in this tiny take-out pizzeria, but you can eat what is considered to be Rome's finest pizza. Master *pizzaiolo*, Gabriele Bonci, uses organic flour for his slow-rise product and then tops the crust with not only classic mixes but wonderfully inventive flavors of his own.

🔲 A3/B4 ✉ Via della Meloria 43 ☎ 06 3974 5416 🕐 Mon–Sat 11–10, Sun 12–4, 6–10 Ⓜ Cipro 🚌 49, 490, 492

LA PRATOLINA €

pizzeriaalapratolina.it

Pizzas here are called *pinsa* in homage to their oval shape, a throwback apparently to bread in ancient Rome. The dough is slow-rise, the wood-fired oven lavastone, and the 37 varieties of toppings range from the classic to the innovative. There are also salads, *crocchette* and antipasti.

🔲 C3 ✉ Via degli Scipioni 248 ☎ 06 3600 4409 🕐 Mon–Sat 7pm–midnight Ⓜ Lepanto/Ottaviano 🚌 30, 70, 81, 87, 130, 280

RESTAURANT ETIQUETTE

Italians have a strong sense of how to behave, which applies in restaurants as much as anywhere. It is considered bad form to order only one course in more sophisticated restaurants—if that is what you want, go to a pizzeria or trattoria.

PRISCILLA €

trattoria-romana.it

This small, family-run trattoria offers classic Roman dishes, including *carciofi alla romana* (artichokes) and *pappardelle al sugo di cinghiale* (large pasta ribbons with wild boar sauce).

🔲 Off map at K9 ✉ Via Appia Antica 68 ☎ 06 513 6379 🕐 Mon–Sat 12–3, 7–11.30; closed part of Feb and Aug

RISTORANTE SIBILLA €€€

ristorantesibilla.com

This restaurant enjoys a glorious setting by Tivoli's circular Temple of Vesta. Dishes might include *cannelloni alle tre carni* (cannelloni with a three-meat filling) and *agnello scottadito con la cicoria* (grilled lamb with chicory).

✉ Via della Sibilla 50, Tivoli ☎ 0774 335281 🕐 Tue–Sun 12.30–3, 7.30–10.30

SAN TEODORO €€€

st-teodoro.it

This established restaurant specializes in fish and seafood. Dine alfresco on traditional delights and lighter dishes. Reserve ahead.

🔲 H7 ✉ Via dei Fienili, 49–51 ☎ 06 678 0933 🕐 Mon–Sat 12.50–3.30, 7.50–11 🚌 C3, H, 30, 44, 63, 81 and other services to Via Petroselli

SANT'EUSTACHIO €

santeustachioilcaffe.it

Excellent coffee is served inside and out at one of Rome's best cafés, accompanied by tasty treats. It also sells beans, capsules, ground coffee and coffee-based chocolates for you to take home.

🔲 F5 ✉ Piazza Sant'Eustachio 82 ☎ 06 6880 2048 🕐 Daily 8.30am–1am (Sat until 2am) 🚌 30, 70, 81, 87, 130 to Corso del Rinascimento

Breakfast in Rome is washed down with a cappuccino or the longer and milkier *caffè latte*. At other times espresso (*un caffè*), a short kick-start of caffeine, is the coffee of choice or *caffè macchiato*, with a drop of milk—Italians never drink cappuccino after lunch or dinner. Decaffeinated coffee is *caffè Hag* and iced coffee *caffè freddo*.

SILVIO ALLA SUBURRA €

This simple restaurant, also known as Osteria della Suburra, is in a quiet street a few minutes' walk from the Colosseum. Pastas are homemade and there's a good house wine from the Frascati Hills.
➕ J6 ✉ Via Urbana 67–69 ☎ 06 486531 🕐 Tue–Sun 12.45–3, 7–11 🚇 Cavour

SORA LELLA €€–€€€

trattoriasoralella.it
Founded by the actress Sora Lella, and now presided over by her son and nephews, this is a former trattoria on the Isola Tiberina. Enjoy Roman cooking, with menu and daily specials. The *gnocchi all' amatriciana* are excellent.
➕ G7 ✉ Via di Ponte Quattro Capi 16 ☎ 06 686 1601 🕐 Daily 12.30–3, 7.30–11 🚌 H, 23, 63, 280 to Lungotevere dei Cenci or 23, 125, 280 to Lungotevere degli Anguillara

LA TAZZA D'ORO €

tazzadorocoffeeshop.com
At this long-established coffee house, roasting is done on the premises and you can sample one of Rome's finest *espressi*. Stand at the old-fashioned counter or take a seat for a shot, before picking up some beans, ground coffee or specialty chocolate to take home.
➕ G5 ✉ Via degli Orfani 84 ☎ 06 678 9792 🕐 Mon–Sat 7am–8pm, Sun 10.30–7.15 🚌 30, 70, 87, 116, 186 to Corso del Rinascimento

TRE SCALINI €

trescalini.it
This long-established bar and restaurant is set on Piazza Navona, its tables spilling onto the square itself. It's famous for its *tartufo*, an ice cream truffle of extraordinary richness and sophistication.
➕ F5 ✉ Piazza Navona 30–35 ☎ 06 6880 1996 🕐 Sun–Fri 10am–midnight, Sat 10am–3am (shorter hours in winter) 🚌 30, 70, 87 and other services to Corso del Rinascimento

VECCHIA ROMA €€

ristorantevecchiaroma.com
Popularity has not spoiled this pretty, predominantly fish restaurant located at the heart of the Ghetto, with outdoor dining in summer on the picturesque piazza terrace or in the 18th-century interior.
➕ G6 ✉ Piazza dei Campitelli 18 ☎ 06 686 4604 🕐 Mon, Tue, Thu–Sun 12.30–3, 8–11; closed 3 weeks in Aug 🚌 44, 46, 60 and other services to Piazza Venezia or Via del Teatro di Marcello

ZARAZÀ €

trattoriazaraza.it
If you're in Frascati, come here for tasty, traditional Roman dishes cooked with a light touch, on the terrace or in one of the attractive dining rooms.
✉ Via Regina Margherita 45, Frascati ☎ 06 942 2053 🕐 Tue–Sun 12.30–2.30, 7.30–10.30; closed Sun 7.30–10.30 Oct–May and 3 weeks in Aug

EAT

Sleep

With options ranging from the luxurious to simple budget hotels, Rome has accommodations to suit everyone. In this section establishments are listed alphabetically.

SLEEP

Introduction

Accommodations in Rome range from opulent, traditional grandeur, through sleek modernity aimed at business travelers, to quirky boutique-style hotels, family-run bed-and-breakfasts and simple hostels for pilgrims.

Location, Location

Accommodations are scattered right across the city, with the most expensive choices along and around Via Vittorio Veneto, mid-range in other parts of the historical central core and budget places near Termini station. What to expect in terms of price and quality depends largely on location. Staying in the *centro storico* you are close to all of Rome's sights, but also to its sounds. Narrow streets and tall buildings tend to amplify the noise. Quiet places can be found, on the edge of the popular areas or in hotels with double glazing. If you value your sleep, book a room in the quieter Aventino, Celio or Prati districts. You will have to travel, but public transport is inexpensive, and hotels are often cheaper than in the heart of the city.

What You Get for Your Money

The familiar star system operates in Italy, with five stars denoting the highest standard of comfort, luxury and facilities. A one-star hotel has few facilities and frequently does not include a private bathroom. Normally both television and telephone will be in the lobby. These establishments tend not to accept credit cards and do not have a 24-hour desk service.

PEAK SEASONS

Reserve well in advance, especially if your stay is over the peak periods, which tend to be the greater part of the year. January to March and August are the least crowded months and you should be able to get some deals in this period—consult hotel websites. If you arrive without a reservation, do ask to see the room before you commit.

From the top: The pretty, ivy-covered Raphaël; entrance of the Hotel Trastevere; help with the luggage; Hotel de Russie

SLEEP

Directory

The Ancient City

Mid-Range
Bolivar
Celio
Nerva
Luxury
Capo d'Africa

Central Rome

Budget
Navona
Pomezia
Smeraldo
Mid-Range
Abruzzi
Albergo Cesari
Campo de' Fiori
Due Torri
La Residenza in Farnese
Luxury
Raphaël

Trastevere and the South

Budget
Trastevere

Northern Rome

Budget
Hotel Panda
Le Petit Real
Mid-Range
Casa Howard
Locarno
Manfredi
Quirinale
Luxury
Hassler-Villa Medici
Hotel de Russie
Regina Hotel Baglioni

Sleeping A–Z

PRICES

Prices are approximate and based on a double room for one night.

€€€	over €300
€€	€150–€300
€	under €150

ABRUZZI €€

hotelabruzzi.it

It's all about location at this hotel, a stone's throw from the Pantheon—some rooms have views of its facade. The stylish rooms are clean-cut and simple, decorated with huge photographic views of Rome on the white walls. It can be noisy, but it's superbly sited.

🔁 F5 ⊠ Piazza della Rotonda 69 ☎ 06 9784 1351 🚌 40, 46, 62, 64, 70, 81, 87 to Largo di Torre Argentina

ALBERGO CESARI €€€

albergocesari.it

Cesari has a loyal clientele, elegant rooms and a fabulous roof garden/terrace. There's been a hotel here since 1787—at the heart of the historic city.

🔁 G5 ⊠ Via di Pietra 89a ☎ 06 674 9701 🚌 C3, 51, 62, 63, 80, 83, 85 to Via del Corso

BOLIVAR €€

bolivarhotel.eu

This four-star hotel is perfectly positioned for sights of the Ancient City, in a quiet alley just off busy

Via IV Novembre. There are 30 rooms, some larger than others, and the glass-walled breakfast room has attractive views.

🔢 H6 ✉ Via della Cordonata 6, between Via IV Novembre and Via XXIV Maggio
☎ 06 679 1614 🚇 Barberini 🚌 H, 40, 60, 64, 70, 170 to Via IV Novembre or Via Nazionale

CAMPO DE' FIORI €€

hotelcampodefiori.com

This hotel is close to Campo de' Fiori. The 27 small rooms vary in decor, from exposed brick to bright red and green colors. The roof garden is a pleasant bonus.

🔢 F6 ✉ Via del Biscione 6 ☎ 06 6880 6865 🚌 40, 46, 62, 64 to Corso Vittorio Emanuele II

CAPO D'AFRICA €€€

hotelcapodafrica.com

Close to the Colosseum, this designer boutique hotel boasts sleek contemporary decor, with sunny, bright shades and displays of Italian modern art.

🔢 K7 ✉ Via Capo d'Africa 54 ☎ 06 772 801 🚇 Colosseo

The Hotel de Russie

SLEEP

CASA HOWARD €€

casahoward.com

Split into two houses, both near the Piazza di Spagna, the owners of this charming accommodation pride themselves on their very personal service, which combines with the comfortable and imaginatively decorated rooms to provide a special Roman experience. The location is excellent for shopping and the sights near the Spanish Steps and Trevi Fountain.

🔢 G4 ✉ Via Capo le Case 18 ☎ 06 6992 4555 🚇 Spagna 🚌 117 to Via dei Due Macelli or all services to Via del Tritone

CELIO €€

hotelcelio.com

In an enviable spot close to the Colosseum and the Forum, this stylish and funky hotel has 19 spacious rooms, each distinguished by large frescoes of Renaissance themes. Rooms are equipped with the latest amenities and those on the upper floor have Jacuzzis.

🔢 J7 ✉ Via dei Santissimi Quattro 35/c ☎ 06 7049 5333 🚇 Colosseo

DUE TORRI €€

hotelduetorriroma.com

You can walk from here to the main sites, some great shopping and a plethora of restaurants. Rooms, spread over five floors (there's an elevator), are smallish but comfortable and the public spaces are furnished with fine antiques and old prints. Fourth- and fifth-floor rooms have balconies or terraces.

🔢 F5 ✉ Vicolo del Leonetto 23–25 ☎ 06 6880 6956 🚌 30, 70, 81, 87 to Lungotevere Marzio or Corso del Rinascimento

HASSLER-VILLA MEDICI €€€

hotelhasslerroma.com

You'll find this well-located, long-time jet-set and VIP haunt just above the Spanish Steps and close to the Colosseum, the Trevi Fountain and Piazza di Spagna. Rooms vary considerably according to price, but all guests have access to the stunning roof terrace restaurant and garden bar. Check the website for their regular offers.

🔲 H4 ✉ Piazza Trinità dei Monti 6 ☎ 06 699 340 🚇 Spagna 🚌 117

HOTEL PANDA €–€€

hotelpanda.it

Just a few steps from classy Piazza di Spagna and the Spanish Steps, the Hotel Panda is excellent value in this pricey area. Housed in a 19th-century palazzo, rooms may be oddly shaped in some cases, but they're clean and bright. Breakfast, although not included in the price, is served in the hotel's coffee bar.

🔲 G3 ✉ Via della Croce 35 ☎ 06 678 0179 🚇 Spagna

HOTEL DE RUSSIE €€€

roccofortehotels.com

A glorious hotel just off Piazza del Popolo distinguished by its modern and stylish design. The rooms are calm and bright, and most have views of the delightful gardens, a lovely spot to dine alfresco.

🔲 F3 ✉ Via del Babuino 9 ☎ 06 328 881 🚇 Flaminio 🚌 117 to Piazza del Popolo

NOISE

Noise is a fact of life in every Roman hotel, whatever the price category. Surveys have shown Rome to be the noisiest city in Europe. It is difficult to escape the cacophony entirely (unless the hotel is air-conditioned and windows are double-glazed), but to lessen the potential racket you should avoid rooms overlooking main thoroughfares and the area around Termini in favor of rooms looking out onto parks or obscure back streets. Also ask for rooms away from the front of the hotel or facing onto a central courtyard (cortile).

LOCARNO €€

hotellocarno.com

In a quietish side street close to Piazza del Popolo, this hotel has genuine 1920s art nouveau decor and period furniture, with a feel of old-world elegance, along with nice touches such as an open fire in winter and a garden and delightful roof terrace. Ask for the better rooms in the eastern annexe, not the downbeat rooms in the main building.

🔲 F3 ✉ Via della Penna 22 ☎ 06 361 0841 🚇 Flaminio 🚌 C3, 301, 628 to Passeggiata di Ripetta, or 301, 628 to Lungotevere in Augusta

MANFREDI €€

hotelmanfredi.it

The creeper-clad facade of this welcoming, family-run hotel, just off Piazza di Spagna, fronts a classically comfortable and traditional type of accommodation. Rooms

SLEEP

AGENCIES

A good source of all kinds of accommodations, from hotels to bed-and-breakfasts in all price ranges, is Enjoy Rome (☎ 06 445 1843 or 06 8837 3403, enjoyrome.com). The company also offers walking and specialist tours.

are sometimes on the small side, but all beautifully furnished and equipped, and the buffet breakfast should keep you going for hours.

🔲 G3 ✉ Via Margutta 61 ☎ 06 320 7676 🚇 Spagna 🚌 119 to Piazza di Spagna

NAVONA €

hotelnavona.com

Rooms are well-sized at this friendly hotel, beautifully situated close to Rome's finest piazza. There are good deals early every month, breakfast included, but expect to pre-pay on these. Remember that rooms facing the street are likely to be noisy at night.

🔲 F5 ✉ Via dei Sediari 8 ☎ 06 6830 1252 🚌 30, 70, 81, 87, 130, 492 to Corso del Rinascimento

NERVA €€

hotelnerva.com

In an unbeatable position for the sights of the Ancient City, the Nerva is one of only a few hotels that are within a stone's throw of the Roman Forum. Renovated modern rooms, some with original features, amiable service and a warm welcome await.

🔲 H6 ✉ Via Tor de' Conti 3–4 ☎ 06 678 1835 or 06 679 3764 🚇 Colosseo or Cavour 🚌 60, 85, 87, 175 and all other services to Via dei Fori Imperiali, Piazza Venezia or Via IV Novembre-Via Nazionale

LE PETIT REAL €

This 3-star hotel in the historic center of Rome pays real attention to detail. The beautifully furnished rooms combine gleaming bedsteads with crystal chandeliers and leather armchairs with plasma-screen TV and big walk-in showers.

🔲 K5 ✉ Via Cavour 58 ☎ 06 482 3566 🚇 Cavour or Termini

POMEZIA €

hotelpomezia.it

Near Piazza Navona and Campo de' Fiori, this modestly comfortable hotel is traditionally furnished and decorated. All rooms have private bathrooms, and there's a roof terrace and small bar. There is a specially adapted room for people with disabilities, but no elevator.

🔲 F6 ✉ Via dei Chiavari 12–15 ☎ 06 686 1371 🚌 46, 62, 64 to Corso Vittorio Emanuele II or 8, 46, 62, 64, 70, 80 to Largo di Torre Argentina

QUIRINALE €€€

hotelquirinale.it

Composers such as Puccini and Verdi have stayed at the charming four-star Quirinale. The high-ceilinged rooms are sensitively refurbished in the neoclassical style, with chandeliers, parquet floors, early Empire furnishings and huge bathrooms. Breakfast,

WHAT TO PAY

Hotels are classified by the Italian state into five categories from one star (basic) to five stars (luxury). The prices each can charge are set by law and must be displayed in the room (you will usually find them on the door). However, prices within a hotel can vary from room to room (and some hotels have off- and peak-season rates). If a room is too expensive, do not be afraid to ask for a less expensive one. Watch for extras like air-conditioning and obligatory breakfasts. Single rooms cost about two-thirds the price of doubles, and to have an extra bed in a room adds 35 percent to the bill. Note that a 2-star hotel might have as much, if not more, charm than a 4-star hotel.

SLEEP

Rome's peak season runs from Easter to October, but the city's hotels (in all categories) are almost invariably busy. Go online, or call if your language skills are good, well in advance to reserve a room (most receptionists speak some English, French or German). Use a credit card if possible to make the booking as it's more likely to give you protection against any fraud. Reconfirm a few days before your trip. If you arrive without a reservation then get to a hotel early in the morning; by afternoon most vacated rooms will have been snapped up. Don't accept rooms from touts at Stazione Termini.

which is taken in the shaded loggia overlooking the courtyard, is a delight.

🚪 J4 ✉ Via Nazionale 7 ☎ 06 4707 Ⓡ Repubblica

RAPHAËL €€€

raphaelhotel.com

This charming, ivy-covered hotel is hidden away in the heart of the *centro storico*. There's a wide range of room types and sizes, but the main draw is the roof-top dining terrace with its views over the cupolas of the cityscape.

🚪 F5 ✉ Largo Febo 2 ☎ 06 682 831 🚌 30, 70, 81, 87, 130 to Corso del Rinascimento

REGINA HOTEL BAGLIONI €€€

baglionihotels.com

Murano glass chandeliers, silk tapestries and marble bathrooms are some of the luxury fixtures and fittings in this Liberty-style hotel. The eighth-floor Sala Belvedere has glass walls and a sun roof with splendid views. Service and attention to detail are exemplary.

🚪 H3 ✉ Via Vittorio Veneto 72 ☎ 06 421 111 Ⓡ Barberini

LA RESIDENZA IN FARNESE €€

residenzafarneseroma.it

This 4-star hotel is located in a superb position in an ivy-hung

alley and in the shadow of the great Palazzo Farnese. Originally part of a former convent, the rooms in this centuries-old building vary from modest former nuns' cells with small bathrooms to large, pastel-decorated salons.

🚪 E6 ✉ Via del Mascherone 59 ☎ 06 6821 0980 🚌 23, 280 to Lungotevere dei Tebaldi

SMERALDO €

smeraldoroma.com

A great central location on an atmospheric backstreet not far from Campo de' Fiori and excellent value for money make this hotel a good choice. All rooms have bathrooms, though some are quite small; some have balconies and there's a lovely roof terrace.

🚪 F6 ✉ Vicolo dei Chiodaroli–Via dei Chiavari ☎ 06 687 5929 🚌 46, 62, 64 to Corso Vittorio Emanuele II or 8, 46, 62, 64, 70, 81 to Largo di Torre Argentina

TRASTEVERE €

hoteltrastevere.net

Prices vary according to room size here, but all offer good value in a central and attractive location. This hotel is popular with Italians; the bed and breakfast offer is a particularly good deal.

🚪 E7 ✉ Via Luciano Manara 24a–25 ☎ 06 581 4713 🚌 H, 8, 780 to Piazza Sonnino or Viale di Trastevere

SLEEP

Need to Know

**This section takes you through all the
practical aspects of your trip to make it run
more smoothly and to give you confidence
before you go and while you are there.**

NEED TO KNOW

Planning Ahead

WHEN TO GO

The best time to visit Rome is April to early June or mid-September to October, when the weather is not uncomfortably hot. Easter weekend is very busy. Many restaurants and businesses close for the entire month of August. January and February are the quietest months.

TIME

Italy is one hour ahead of GMT in winter, six hours ahead of New York and nine hours ahead of Los Angeles.

TEMPERATURE

JAN	FEB	MAR	APR	MAY	JUN	JUL	AUG	SEP	OCT	NOV	DEC
44°F	46°F	52°F	58°F	64°F	74°F	79°F	77°F	72°F	64°F	55°F	48°F
7°C	8°C	11°C	14°C	18°C	23°C	26°C	25°C	22°C	18°C	13°C	9°C

Spring (March to May) can be muggy. It can be rainy in March, and through to May.
Summer (June to August) is hot and dry, with sudden thunderstorms, especially in August. July and August are uncomfortably hot.
Autumn (September to November) is mixed but can produce crisp days with clear skies.
Winter (December to February) is short and moderately cold.

WHAT'S ON

January *La Befana* (6 Jan): Epiphany celebrations; fair and market in Piazza Navona.
February *Carnevale* (week before Lent): Costume festivities; parties on Shrove Tuesday.
March *Festa di San Giuseppe* (19 Mar): Street stalls in the Trionfale area north of the Vatican.
April *Good Friday* (Mar/Apr): Procession of the Cross at 9pm to the Colosseum, led by the Pope.
Easter Sunday: The Pope addresses the assembled crowds at noon in Piazza di San Pietro.
May *Primo Maggio* (1 May): Free rock concert on Labor Day in Piazza

San Giovanni in Laterano, featuring both Italian and international artists.
International Horse Show (early May): Concorso Ippico in Villa Borghese.
June *Festa della Repubblica* (2 Jun): Military parade along Via dei Fori Imperiali.
Lungo il Tevere (2nd week Jun–Jul): Art, culture, music and food festival on the banks of the Tiber.
August *Ferragosto* (15 Aug): Feast of the Assumption; everything closes for at least the day.
September *Art Fair*: One of several in Via Margutta.
Sagra dell'Uva (Sep): Wine and harvest festival in towns of Castelli Romani.

October *Roma Europa*: International dance and drama festival October to November and beyond.
November *Ognissanti* (1–2 Nov): All Saints' Day.
Rome International Film Festival: Various venues (9–12 Nov in 2017).
Festa di Santa Cecilia (22 Nov): In the catacombs and church of Santa Cecilia in Trastevere.
December *Festa della Madonna Immacolata* (8 Dec): Pope and other dignitaries leave flowers at the statue of the Madonna in Piazza di Spagna.
Christmas Eve Midnight Mass: The most striking are at Santa Marias Maggiore and in Aracoeli.

ROME ONLINE

060608.it
Rome's official website for tourist information has excellent practical information on the city.

adr.it
The official site of Rome's main airports, Leonardo da Vinci and Ciampino, with useful contacts and details of transport links to the city.

w2.vatican.va and museivaticani.va
Vatican City's polished official websites offer multilingual information on the Vatican Museums, the Sistine Chapel and St. Peter's, a calendar of religious events, an online version of its official newspaper and other general information on the Vatican.

comune.roma.it
Aimed primarily at residents, the official website of Rome's city council contains transport and other useful general information.

romaclick.com
This site is dedicated to accommodation deals and airport transfers, and offers a user-friendly accommodation reservation service with last-minute reductions.

romeguide.it
An Italian-based site with a wealth of daily updated information; use it for reserving museum passes and to find out what's on.

enjoyrome.com
This friendly English-language site is run from Rome and has a quirkier approach than most; use it for general information, as well as useful tips on discovering Rome on foot and by public transport. It also has excellent links and daily updates.

museionline.it
An informative, easy-to-navigate site that will fill you in on what the city's museums have to offer. Lots of practical information, but opening times and prices are not always current.

TRAVEL SITES

atac.roma.it
Rome's bus company website gives every scrap of information about public transport, including maps and how to buy the best ticket for your needs.

capitolium.org
Devoted to the Roman and Imperial forums, this site includes a wide range of historical material, including reconstructions of how the forums might have originally looked.

catacombe.roma.it
The official site of Rome's San Callisto catacombs.

fodors.com
A travel-planning site where you can research prices, book tickets, cars and rooms, and ask questions; links to other sites.

INTERNET ACCESS
Much of central Rome is covered by a free, city-funded wireless network. New users need to register and enter—and have—a mobile phone number. For further information ☎ 06 6919 0720, romawireless.com.

Getting There

VISAS AND INSURANCE

Check visa and passport requirements before traveling, see gov.uk or it.usembassy.gov.
EU citizens with an EHIC card are entitled to the same cover for medical treatment as Italian residents (for which they may still have to pay); insurance to cover illness and theft is still strongly advised. Visitors from outside the EU should check their insurance coverage and, if necessary, buy a supplementary policy.

TIPS

● Avoid taxi and hotel touts who will approach you at the airport. Use only licensed (white) taxis. Fares are fixed for most destinations in the city center.

● Buy your return (round-trip) train ticket online (trenitalia.com) or when you arrive at Fiumicino. The lines are much longer at Termini, and the ticket will not become valid until you stamp it on your return journey.

● You will find suitcases with wheels a godsend at Fiumicino. It is quite some distance between baggage reclaim and the exit, and for some stretches you cannot use a baggage trolley, particularly on the homeward journey.

AIRPORTS

There are direct flights into Rome from Europe and North America to Leonardo da Vinci (Fiumicino) and Ciampino airports. Visitors from Europe can also arrive by rail to Stazione Termini, or by bus to Stazione Tiburtina.

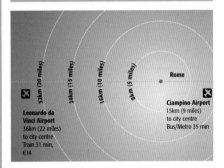

32km (20 miles) | 24km (15 miles) | 16km (10 miles) | 8km (5 miles) | Rome

Leonardo da Vinci Airport
36km (22 miles) to city centre
Train 31 min, €14

Ciampino Airport
15km (9 miles) to city centre
Bus/Metro 35 min

FROM LEONARDO DA VINCI AIRPORT

Scheduled flights arrive at this airport 36km (22 miles) southwest of the city, better known as Fiumicino (tel switchboard 06 65951). The website for both main Rome airports is adr.it. The most efficient way to reach the heart of Rome from the airport is by rail into Stazione Termini. Trains leave every 15–60 minutes (6.23am–11.23pm) at 8, 15, 23 and 38 minutes past the hour at peak times and take about 30 minutes. Catch the Leonardo Express service direct to Termini, not the service via Fara Sabina. Buses (sitbusshuttle.it) depart from Terminal 3 (8.30am–12.30am) and take up to 50 minutes to Rome's Termini and Tiburtina train stations. Taxis take from 30 minutes to two hours depending on traffic, and are expensive (€48 set fare, maximum four passengers, including luggage, to points within the Aurelian Walls). Take only licensed cabs (white) or a prepaid car with driver available from desks in Terminal 1 or Terminal 3.

FROM CIAMPINO

This smaller airport, which handles mostly low-cost and charter flights, is 15km (9 miles) southeast of the city. There are good facilities but the airport does not have a direct rail link to the heart of Rome. To get there take a 15-minute bus journey by ATRAL bus to the Metro (underground) station at Anagnina, then the 20-minute journey to Termini on Metro line A. Taxis take 30 to 40 minutes and cost around €30. Bus shuttles (terravision.eu, sitbusshuttle.it) serve various no-frills and other airlines' flights and run to Termini (from €4 one-way, €8 round-trip booked online, otherwise €6/€11 at the airport).

ARRIVING BY BUS

Most long-distance buses terminate at Tiburtina, to the northeast of the city. Although the station is some way out of the city, it is well served by the Metro (line B) to Termini or Colosseo and by local trains and numerous bus services (for example No. 492 to the center). Eurolines run buses from more than 100 European cities. For details of routes, times and tickets, visit their website (eurolines.it).

ARRIVING BY CAR

In the days of the empire, all roads led to Rome, but in these modern times, all roads lead to the Gran Raccordo Anulare, known as the GRA. This 70km (43-mile) road encircles the city, and is always busy. From Fiumicino airport, take the Autostrada Roma Fiumicino, which leads to the GRA. If you are coming from Ciampino you will need to follow the Via Appia Nuova. From Florence or Pisa, take the A1, also known as the Autostrada del Sole. Visitors arriving from Naples should also use the A1, while those coming from Abruzzo or the Adriatic coast should follow the A24. Wherever you join the GRA, make sure you know which exit you need; your hotel can tell you which one is best.

ARRIVING BY RAIL

Most trains arrive and depart from Stazione Termini, convenient for most of central Rome. Taxis and buses leave from the station forecourt, Piazza dei Cinquecento. For train information it's best to look online; trenitalia.com has an English-language site or call 89 20 21.

DRIVING PERMIT

If you are driving and staying in central Rome, you will need a permit to drive in the city. If you are staying in a hotel, the staff can arrange this for you.

LONG-TERM PARKING

If you are arriving by car, but don't want to use it in Rome, you can leave it in the long-term parking area *(Lunga Sosta)* at Fiumicino airport. Long stay costs from €18 daily (from €5.50 if booked online at easy-parking.adr.it) for 24 hours or €69 for seven days. Short-stay in "Multipiano E" costs €30 (from €19 online) daily or €5 hourly.

CAR RENTAL

All major rental firms, and some local ones, have desks at both airports and in town. Car rental is expensive in Italy and you can often get a better deal if you arrange it in advance. The minimum age for renting a car is between 21 and 25 (depending on the company), and you will need to have held a driver's license for at least a year. Most firms require a credit card as a deposit. Accident rates are high in Rome, so make sure you have adequate insurance cover. Most car rental contracts include breakdown cover.

Getting Around

VISITORS WITH DISABILITIES

Rome is not an easy place for visitors with physical disabilities. However, the Vatican City has ramps and elevators and some hotels have rooms for visitors with disabilities. Staff at airports, museums and places of interest are willing to help and taxis usually accept wheelchairs, although it is a good idea to phone ahead. Metro line B is generally accessible (apart from Circo Massimo, Colosseo and Cavour) but Metro line A and most buses are not. Transit site atac.roma.it has an English page and links with further detailed information.

Sage Traveling (☎ 888/645 7920 in US, sagetraveling. com) is an excellent English-language resource. For details (but mostly in Italian) contact CO.IN (coin-sociale.it), which can give advice and organize transport in advance. Roma per Tutti (romapertutti.it) provide information on accessibility to buildings and other facilities. In the US also go to the Society for the Advancement of Travel and Hospitality (SATH, ☎ 212/447 7284, sath.org).

BUSES

Service is frequent and inexpensive on Rome's mostly green or red-gray regional and blue suburban buses run by ATAC/COTRAL (map ref K4, Piazza dei Cinquecento, tel 06 57003, atac. roma.it and cotralspa.it, Mon–Sat 8–8, Metro Termini).

The buses are often crowded and slow. Buy BIT tickets *(Biglietto Integrato a Tempo;* €1.50*)* before boarding, from tobacconists, shops and automatic machines displaying an ATAC sticker. Your ticket must be stamped at the rear of the bus or tram, and is valid for any number of bus rides and one Metro ride within the next 100 minutes. Roma 24 one-day (€7), Roma 48 2-day (€12.50), Roma 72 3-day (€18), Roma CIS 7-day (€24) passes and an èRoma pass (atac.roma.it) are available. Validate these the first time they are used. Services run 5.30am–11.30pm, depending on the route.

The night service consists of buses on key routes midnight–5.30am; night buses have a conductor selling tickets.

Remember to enter buses by back doors and to leave by middle doors (if you have a pass or validated ticket with unexpired time you can also use the front doors).

Buy several tickets at once as some outlets close early. There are large fines if you are caught without a ticket. Bus stops *(fermate)* list routes and bus numbers, but bear in mind that one-way streets often force buses to return along different routes. Bus number 64 is especially notorious for pickpockets and work to extend Rome's Metro means some bus services may follow temporary diversions.

USEFUL SERVICES

● 23 Piazza del Risorgimento (for the Vatican Museums)–Trastevere–Piramide.
● 75 Termini–Roman Forum–Colosseum–Piramide.
● 40, 64 Termini–Piazza Venezia–close to Piazza San Pietro/St. Peter's.
● 110 Open Sightseeing service from Stazione Termini to the Colosseum and other key monuments.

NEED TO KNOW

● 81 Piazza del Risorgimento (Vatican Museums)–Piazza Venezia–Circo Massimo.
● 117 Circular minibus service in the historic center including Piazza del Popolo–Via del Corso–Via Cavour–Roman Forum–Colosseum–San Giovanni in Laterano.

SUBWAY

Rome's Metro (romametropolitane.it), has three lines, A, B and C. A and B intersect at Stazione Termini. Mainly a commuter service and of limited use in the city, it is good for trans-city rides. Station entrances are marked by a large M and each displays a map of the network. Services run 5.30am to 11.30pm (12.30am Saturday). Tickets are valid for one ride (or get a BIT, see "Buses") and can be bought from tobacconists, bars and shops displaying ATAC or COTROL stickers, and from machines at stations—have euro coins handy.

TAXIS

Official taxis are white, with an official number and a Taxi sign on the roof. Use only these and refuse touts at Fiumicino, Termini and elsewhere. Drivers are not supposed to stop on the streets so it is difficult to hail a cab. Taxis congregate at stands, indicated by blue signs printed with Taxi. Make sure the taxi meter is reset when you start your journey (one part of the meter will display the minimum fare starting rate). Taxi ranks are available in the area at Termini, Piazza Sidney Sonnino, Pantheon, Piazza di Spagna and Piazza San Silvestro.

When calling a taxi, the company will give you a taxi code name, a number and the time it will take to get to you. The meter starts running as soon as they are called. Companies include: Samarcanda, tel 06 5551, 065551.it; and Cooperativa Radiotaxi (tel 06 3570, 3570.it). The minimum fare is valid for 3km (2.5 miles) or the first 9 minutes of a ride. Surcharges are levied between 10pm and 7am, all day Sunday, on national holidays, for airport trips (€48 set fare to or from Fiumicino, €30 to or from Ciampino) and for each piece of luggage larger than 35x25x50cm (13x9x19in).

HANDY HINT

The *Biglietto Integrato Giornaliero* (BIG, Roma 24H, €7) is valid for a day's unlimited travel on ATAC and COTRAL buses, the Metro and suburban trains (except to Fiumicino airport). *The Carta Integrata Settimanale* pass, or CIS, (€24) is valid for a week, as for Roma 24H tickets (see above). BiPiù can be used as a payment method and ticket in conjunction with smart phones.

LOST PROPERTY

Report lost or stolen property at a police station, which will issue a signed declaration for insurance purposes. The main police station is the Questura
✉ Via San Vitale 15
☎ 06 46861
ATAC lost property
✉ Circonvallazione Ostiense 191 ☎ 06 6769 3214 🕓 Tue, Wed, Fri 8–1, Thu 8.30–5
Metro lost property
Line A ☎ 06 4695 7068; Line B ☎ 06 5735 2264 🕓 Mon, Wed, Fri 9.30–12.30
COTRAL lost property
Inquire at the route's origin, file online (Oggetti Smarriti link at cotralspa.it) ☎ 800 174 471 or 06 7205 7205
Airport lost property
☎ Ciampino 06 6595 9565, Fiumicino 06 6595 3313

Essential Facts

MONEY

The euro is the official currency of Italy. Banknotes come in denominations of 5, 10, 20, 50, 100, 200 and 500 euros and coins in 1, 2, 5, 10, 20, 50 cents and 1 and 2 euros.

TOURIST INFORMATION

● Azienda di Promozione Turistica di Roma:
✉ Via Parigi 11 🕐 Mon–Sat 8am–7.30pm
● Information kiosks (daily 9.30–7) are at:
✉ Piazza delle Cinque Lune (Piazza Navona)
✉ Palazzo delle Esposizioni, Via Nazionale
✉ Lungotevere Castel Sant'Angelo-Piazza Pia
Central number for tourist information: ☎ 060608

EMBASSIES

UK
✉ Via XX Settembre 80/A
☎ 06 4220 0001,
gov.uk
US
✉ Via Vittorio Veneto 121
☎ 06 46741,
it.usembassy.gov
Canada
✉ Via Zara 30 ☎ 06 85444 2911, canada international.gc.ca/italy
Spain
✉ Largo Fontanella di Borghese 19 ☎ 06 684 0401, exteriores.gob.es/embajadas/roma

ELECTRICITY

● Current is 220 volts AC, 50 cycles; plugs are the two-round-pin type.

NATIONAL HOLIDAYS

● 1 Jan (New Year's Day)
● 6 Jan (Epiphany)
● Easter Monday
● 25 Apr (Liberation Day)
● 1 May (Labor Day)
● 29 Jun (St. Peter and St. Paul's Day)
● 15 Aug (Assumption)
● 1 Nov (All Saints' Day)
● 8 Dec (Immaculate Conception)
● 25 Dec (Christmas Day)
● 26 Dec (St. Stephen's Day)

NEWSPAPERS AND MAGAZINES

● Many Romans read the Rome-based *Il Messaggero*, and the mainstream and authoritative *Corriere della Sera* or the middle-left and populist *La Repubblica* (which has a special Rome edition). Sports papers (such as *Corriere dello Sport*) and weekly news magazines (such as *Panorama* and *L'Espresso*) are also popular.
● Foreign newspapers can usually be bought after 2.30pm on the day of issue from booths *(edicole)* on and close to Termini, Piazza Colonna, Largo di Torre Argentina, Piazza Navona, Via Vittoria Veneto and close to several tourist sights. European editions of major newspapers are also available.

OPENING HOURS

● Shops: Tue–Sat 8–1, 4–8; Mon 4–8 (with seasonal variations) or, increasingly Mon/Tue–Sat 9.30–7.30 with no lunch break. Food shops open on Monday morning but may close on Thursday afternoon. Some bookshops open on Sundays.
● Restaurants: daily 12.30–3, 7.30–10.30. Many close on Sunday evening and half- or all day Monday. Most bars and restaurants also have a statutory closing day *(riposo settimanale)* and many close for much of August, when Italians go on holiday.

- Churches: variable, but usually daily 7–12, 4.30–7. Most churches close on Sunday afternoon.
- Museums and galleries: vary considerably; usually close on Monday.
- Banks: Mon–Fri 8.30–1.30. Major branches may also open 3–4 and Saturday morning.
- Post offices: Mon–Fri 8.15 or 9–2; Sat 8.15 or 9–12 or 2.

POSTAL SERVICE
- Buy stamps from post offices and tobacconists.
- Post boxes are red and have two slots, one for Rome (marked *Per La Città*) and one for other destinations *(Per Tutte Le Altre Destinazioni)*. Newer boxes, usually blue, are for the priority mail service, or *Posta Prioritaria*.
- Vatican post can be posted only in the Vatican's blue *Poste Vaticane* post boxes. The Vatican postal service is quicker (although tariffs are the same), but stamps can be bought only at the post offices in the Vatican Museums (▷ 26–27) and in Piazza San Pietro, tel 06 6989 0400, Mon–Sat 8.30–6.30.
- Main post office *(Ufficio Postale Centrale)* Piazza San Silvestro 19, tel 06 6973 7216, poste.it, Mon–Fri 8–7 (Aug Mon–Fri 8–2), Sat 8–1.15

TELEPHONES
- Telephone numbers listed in this book include the city area code (06), which must be dialed even when calling within Rome.
- Public telephones are indicated by a red or yellow sign showing a telephone dial and receiver. They are found on the street, in bars and restaurants and in special offices *(Centri Telefoni)* equipped with banks of phones.
- Phones usually accept phone cards *(schede telefoniche)* available from tobacconists, post offices and some bars in a variety of denominations. Break off the card's corner before use.
- To call Italy from the UK, dial 00 39 and from the US or Canada dial 011, followed by 39 (the country code for Italy) then the number, including the relevant city code.

MEDICAL TREATMENT

Emergency rooms at: Ospedale Fatebenefratelli ✉ Isola Tiberina ☎ 06 68371, fatebenefratelli-isolatiberina.it ✉ Viale del Policlinico 155 ☎ 06 49971, policlinicoumberto1.it. The George Eastman Clinic (✉ Viale Regina Elena 287/b ☎ 06 7730 3258) provides an emergency dentist service. No credit cards.

Pharmacies are usually open Mon–Sat 8.30–1, 4–8, but a rotating schedule (displayed on pharmacy doors) ensures at least one is always open. Two central pharmacies are Senato (✉ Corso del Rinascimento 48 ☎ 06 6880 3760), near Piazza Navona, and Internazionale (✉ Piazza Barberini 49 ☎ 06 487 1195), near the Spanish Steps.

EMERGENCY NUMBERS

Police, Fire and Ambulance (general SOS) ☎ 112
Police (Carabinieri) ☎ 112
Central Police ☎ 06 46861
Telephone Information: ☎ 1254 (24 hours), 1254.virgilio.it
International information: ☎ 1254 (8am–10.30pm)
ACI Auto Assistance (car breakdowns): ☎ 803 116, aci.it

Words and Phrases

All Italian words are pronounced as written, with each vowel and consonant sounded. Only the letter *h* is silent, but it modifies the sound of other letters. The letter *c* is hard, as in English cat, except when followed by *i* or *e*, when it becomes the soft *ch* of cello. Similarly, *g* is soft (as in the English giant) when followed by *i* or *e—giardino, gelati*; otherwise hard (as in gas)—*gatto*. Words ending in *o* are almost always masculine in gender (plural: *-i*); those ending in *a* are generally feminine (plural: *-e*). Use the polite second person *(lei)* to speak to strangers and the informal second person *(tu)* to friends or children.

BASICS

yes	*sì*
no	*no*
maybe	*forse*
OK/alright	*va bene*
please	*per favore*
thank you	*grazie*
many thanks	*grazie mille*
you're welcome	*prego*
excuse me!	*mi scusi*
when	*quando*
now	*adesso*
why	*perchè*
who	*chi*
may I/can I	*posso*
good morning	*buon giorno*
good afternoon	*buona sera*
good evening	*buona notte*
hello/good-bye (informal)	*ciao*
hello (on the telephone)	*pronto*
I'm sorry	*mi dispiace*
left/right	*sinistra/destra*
open/closed	*aperto/chiuso*
good/bad	*buono/cattivo*
big/small	*grande/piccolo*
with/without	*con/senza*
more/less	*più/meno*
hot/cold	*caldo/freddo*
do you have?	*avete?*
exit	*uscita*
nothing	*niente*
slow	*piano*
fast	*presto/rapido*

NUMBERS

1	*uno, una*
2	*due*
3	*tre*
4	*quattro*
5	*cinque*
6	*sei*
7	*sette*
8	*otto*
9	*nove*
10	*dieci*
20	*venti*
30	*trenta*
40	*quaranta*
50	*cinquanta*
100	*cento*
1,000	*mille*

COLORS

black	*nero*
brown	*marrone*
pink	*rosa*
red	*rosso*
orange	*arancione*
yellow	*giallo*
green	*verde*
light blue	*celeste*
sky blue	*azzuro*
purple	*viola*
white	*bianco*
gray	*grigio*

EMERGENCIES

help!	*aiuto!*
stop, thief!	*al ladro!*
can you help me, please?	*può aiutarmi, per favore?*
call the police/ an ambulance	*chiami la polizia/un'ambulanza*
I have lost my wallet/passport	*ho perso il mio portafoglio/ il mio passaporto*
where is the police station?	*dov'è il commissariato?*
where is the hospital?	*dov'è l'ospedale?*
I don't feel well	*non mi sento bene*
first aid	*pronto soccorso*

USEFUL PHRASES

how are you? (informal)	*come sta/stai?*
I'm fine	*sto bene*
I do not understand	*non ho capito*
how much is it?	*quant'è?*
do you have a room?	*avete camere libere?*
how much per night?	*quanto costa una notte?*
with bath/shower	*con vasca/doccia*
when is breakfast served?	*a che ora è servita la colazione?*
where is the train/bus station?	*dov'è la stazione ferroviaria/degli autobus?*
excuse me (on bus, train etc)	*mi scusi*
do I have to get off here?	*devo scendere qui?*
where can I buy...?	*dove posso comprare...?*
I would like	*vorrei*
too expensive	*troppo caro*
a table for... please	*un tavolo per... per favore*
excuse me (to attract attention)	*senta*
the bill, please	*il conto, per favore*
we didn't have this	*non abbiamo avuto questo*
where are the toilets?	*dove sono i bagni?*

DAYS/MONTHS

Monday	*lunedì*
Tuesday	*martedì*
Wednesday	*mercoledì*
Thursday	*giovedì*
Friday	*venerdì*
Saturday	*sabato*
Sunday	*Domenica*
January	*gennaio*
February	*febbraio*
March	*marzo*
April	*aprile*
May	*maggio*
June	*giugno*
July	*luglio*
August	*agosto*
September	*settembre*
October	*ottobre*
November	*novembre*
December	*dicembre*

TIME AND PLACE

morning	*mattina*
afternoon	*pomeriggio*
evening	*sera*
night	*notte*
today	*oggi*
tomorrow	*domani*
yesterday	*ieri*
early	*presto*
late	*tardi*
later	*più tardi*
when	*quando*
where	*dove*
Where is...?	*Dov'è...?*
Where are we?	*Dove siamo?*
here	*qui/qua*
there	*lì/là*
near	*vicino*
far	*lontano*
on the right	*a destra*
on the left	*a sinistra*

Index

The Automobile Association would like to thank the following photographers, companies and picture libraries for their assistance in the preparation of this book.

2i–2v AA/A Mockford & Nick Bonetti; 3i, iii AA/A Mockford & Nick Bonetti; 3ii AA/C Sawyer; 3iv AA/Simon McBride; 4–5 AA/A Mockford & Nick Bonetti; 6t The Art Archive/Galleria Borghese Rome/Collection Dagli Orti; 6ct, 6–7b AA/A Mockford & Nick Bonetti; 6cb AA/Dario Miterdiri; 7t AA/A Mockford & Nick Bonetti; 7ct *Apollo & Daphne*, 1622–25 (Marble), Bernini, Gian Lorenzo (1598–1680)/Galleria Borghese, Rome, Italy/Giraudon/The Bridgeman Art Library; 7cb AA/Simon McBride; 8t, 8–9ct AA/Simon McBride; 8cb AA/A Mockford & Nick Bonetti; 8–9b, cb, 9ct AA/C Sawyer; 9t AA/Peter Wilson; 10l Getty Images; 10r AA; 11l AA/Simon McBride; 11r epa european pressphoto agency b.v./Alamy; 12 AA/A Mockford & Nick Bonetti; 14–15 AA/Simon McBride; 15–16 AA/A Mockford & Nick Bonetti; 16–17, 17cr AA/A Mockford & Nick Bonetti; 17tr AA/Simon McBride; 18l Dominic Jones/Alamy; 18–19 Richard Boot/Alamy; 20l AA/Jim Holmes; 20–21l Findlay/Alamy; 21t Gone with the Wind/Alamy; 21c Scott Carruthers/Alamy; 23 AA/A Mockford & Nick Bonetti; 24tl AA/Simon McBride; 24cl, 24–25 AA/Jim Holmes; 25tr, cr AA/C Sawyer; 26tl, cl, 26–27t AA/A Mockford & Nick Bonetti; 26r AA/Simon McBride; 28 AA/A Mockford & Nick Bonetti; 28–29 AA; 29tr Massimo Pizzotti/Alamy; 29cr AA/A Mockford & Nick Bonetti; 30, 30–31 AA/Jim Holmes; 31 *Youth with a Basket of Fruit*, 1594 (oil on canvas), Caravaggio Michelangelo Merisi da (1571–1610)/Galleria Borghese, Rome, Italy/Alinari/The Bridgeman Art Library; 32 AA/C Sawyer; 32–33 AA/A Mockford & Nick Bonetti; 34 Erin Babnik/Alamy; 34–35 AA/A Mockford & Nick Bonetti; 36 AA/Peter Wilson; 36–37t AA/Jim Holmes; 36–37c AA/Peter Wilson; 37tr *Judith and Holofernes*, 1599 (oil on canvas), Caravaggio, Michelangelo Merisi da (1571–1610)/Palazzo Barberini, Rome, Italy/The Bridgeman Art Library; 37cr AA/A Mockford & Nick;Bonetti; 38tl AA/Peter Wilson; 38cl, 38–39 AA/Jim Holmes; 39 *Salome with the Head of St. John the Baptist* (oil on canvas), Solario, Antonio da (fl.1502–14)/Galleria Doria Pamphilj, Rome, Italy/Alinari/The Bridgeman Art Library; 40–41 AA/A Mockford & Nick Bonetti; 42–43, 43tr AA/A Mockford & Nick Bonetti; 43cr AA/Simon McBride; 44, 44–45c, 45tr AA/C Sawyer; 44–45ct AA/Alex Kouprianoff; 45cr AA/Jim Holmes; 46, 46–47c, 47cr AA/A Mockford & Nick Bonetti; 46–47ct AA/Simon McBride; 47tr AA/C Sawyer; 48 dpa picture alliance/Alamy; 48–49 Valery Voennyy; 50, 50–51c, 51tr AA/A Mockford & Nick;Bonetti; 50–51ct, 51cr AA/Jim Holmes; 52–53 AA/A Mockford & Nick Bonetti; 54 AA/Dario Miterdiri; 54–55, 55tr AA/C Sawyer; 55cr image1/Alamy; 56 AA/Jim Holmes; 56–57 Adam Eastland Rome/Alamy; 57tr Vito Arcomano/Alamy; 57cr AA; 58tl, 58–59 AA/A Mockford & Nick Bonetti; 58cl AA/Simon McBride; 59 AA/Alex Kouprianoff; 60–61ct Razvan Cosac/Alamy; 61tr AA/A Mockford & Nick Bonetti; 61br Peter Moulton/Alamy; 62 AA/Dario Miterdiri; 62–63ct AA/Alex Kouprianoff; 62–63cb, 63 AA/Jim Holmes; 64 AA/A Mockford & Nick Bonetti; 66 AA/T Souter; 67bl AA/C Sawyer; 67br AA/A Mockford & Nick Bonetti; 68–69 AA/A Mockford & Nick Bonetti; 70bl AA/A Mockford & Nick Bonetti; 70br Adam Eastland Rome/Alamy; 71bl AA/A Mockford & Nick Bonetti; 71br AA/Alex Kouprianoff; 72bl AA/Jim Holmes;72br AA/A Mockford & Nick Bonetti; 73bl AA/Jim Holmes; 73br AA/A Mockford & Nick Bonetti; 74bl AA/A Mockford & Nick Bonetti; 74br AA/Jim Holmes; 75 AA/A Mockford & Nick Bonetti; 76bl AA/A Mockford & Nick Bonetti; 76br MARKA/Alamy; 77bl AA/C Sawyer; 77br AA/Simon McBride; 78 AA/Simon McBride; 79 AA/A Mockford & Nick Bonetti; 80 AA/Alex Kouprianoff; 82t AA/A Mockford & Nick Bonetti; 82b AA/Dario Miterdiri; 83 AA/A Mockford & Nick Bonetti; 86i–ii, iv AA/A Mockford & Nick Bonetti; 86iii AA/C Sawyer; 86v AA/Alex Kouprianoff; 86vi AA/Dario Miterdiri; 88t AA/Jim Holmes; 88b AA/A Mockford & Nick Bonetti; 89t AA/Dario Miterdiri; 89b AA/A Mockford & Nick Bonetti; 92i AA/Jim Holmes; 92ii AA/Dario Miterdiri; 92iii AA/A Mockford & Nick Bonetti; 92iv AA/Alex Kouprianoff; 92v–vi AA/C Sawyer; 94t, 95 AA/A Mockford & Nick Bonetti; 94b AA/Alex Kouprianoff; 98t AA/Alex Kouprianoff; 98c Ken Welsh/Alamy; 98b AA/Dario Miterdiri; 100–101 AA/A Mockford & Nick Bonetti; 104i, iv–v, vii AA/A Mockford & Nick Bonetti; 104ii–iii AA/Peter Wilson; 104vi AA/Jim Holmes; 106t AA/A Mockford & Nick Bonetti; 106b AA/C Sawyer; 107 AA/A Mockford & Nick Bonetti; 110–111 AA/A Mockford & Nick Bonetti; 112t AA/Jim Holmes; 112b AA/Peter Wilson; 113 AA/A Mockford & Nick Bonetti; 116 AA/C Sawyer; 117–118 AA/A Mockford & Nick Bonetti; 120–121t AA/A Mockford & Nick Bonetti; 120–121ct AA/Dario Miterdiri; 121ctl AA/A Mockford & Nick Bonetti; 120–121cb, 121cbl AA/C Sawyer; 120–121b AA/A Mockford & Nick Bonetti; 123 AA/C Sawyer; 128 AA/A Mockford & Nick Bonetti; 130–131t, ct, cb AA/A Mockford & Nick Bonetti; 131ctl AA/Simon McBride; 131cb Digitalvision; 130–131b AA/James Tims; 133 Brand X Pics; 134 AA/A Mockford & Nick Bonetti; 135 AA/Jim Holmes; 136 Digitalvision; 137 AA/A Mockford & Nick Bonetti; 138 AA/C Sawyer; 140i AA/A Mockford & Nick Bonetti; 140ii AA/Peter Wilson; 140iii AA/C Sawyer; 140iv AA/Terry Harris; 143 AA/A Mockford & Nick Bonetti; 144 AA/C Sawyer; 148 AA/Eric Meacher; 152 AA/A Mockford & Nick Bonetti; 154i–ii AA/C Sawyer; 154iii–iv AA/A Mockford & Nick Bonetti; 156 AA/A Mockford & Nick Bonetti; 160 AA/Peter Wilson.

Every effort has been made to trace the copyright holders, and we apologise in advance for any unintentional omissions or errors. We would be pleased to apply any corrections in a following edition of this publication.

CityPack Rome

Published by AA Publishing, a trading name of AA Media Limited, whose registered office is Fanum House, Basing View, Basingstoke, Hampshire RG21 4EA. Registered number 06112600.

© AA Media Limited 2018
First published 1996
Revised and updated 2015
New edition 2018

Written and updated by Tim Jepson
Series editor Clare Ashton
Design work Liz Baldin
Image retouching and repro Ian Little

Colour separation by AA Digital Department
Printed and bound by Leo Paper Products, China

A CIP catalogue record for this book is available from the British Library.

ISBN 978-0-7495-7938-8

A05542
Maps in this title produced from mapping © MAIRDUMONT / Falk Verlag 2016 and data from openstreetmap.org © OpenStreetMap contributors
Transport map © Communicarta Ltd, UK

Titles in the Series

- Amsterdam
- Bangkok
- Barcelona
- Berlin
- Boston
- Brussels & Bruges
- Budapest
- Dublin
- Edinburgh
- Florence
- Hong Kong
- Istanbul
- Las Vegas
- Lisbon
- London
- Madrid
- Milan
- Munich
- New York
- Orlando
- Paris
- Prague
- Rome
- San Francisco
- Singapore
- Sydney
- Toronto
- Venice
- Vienna
- Washington